The Quest

D1744236

The Quest

Stage One: Elements

Eric Williams

Edward Arnold

The Quest

Stage one: ELEMENTS

Stage two: CREATURES

Stage three: TRIALS

© Eric Williams 1973

First published 1973
by Edward Arnold (Publishers) Ltd.,
25 Hill Street,
London W1X 8LL

ISBN: 0 7131 1749 4

Photoset in 12 on 13 point Lumitype Times New Roman and
Printed in Great Britain by Butler and Tanner Ltd
Frome and London

Introduction

These books are intended for pupils of 11 to 14 and can be used with groups of varied or mixed ability. The books can be used by themselves or in preparation for 'People', a companion volume written for pupils of 14 to 16. They share its concern for flexibility, with chapters divided into three sections, each of which can be used independently to fit in with an individual class's requirements, or used in conjunction with the rest in a continuously developing unit. (Similarly, each book is self-contained, though Stages Two and Three can be used, as their titles imply, to lead on from where the previous Stage ends.) The arrangement and layout have been designed to make it easy for the teacher to weave the parts that he needs into his own scheme. Similarly, the suggestions I make are open-ended: they will be used by classes to a differing extent— it is certainly not necessary to follow up each of the suggestions, and, in any case, some may lead to work development along different lines from those the scheme of these books anticipates, following the interests of each teaching group. For convenience of reference, the work suggested for development from the poems, legends, extracts from children's novels and short stories (as well as a wealth of photographs and drawings, which are not used as mere illustrations but as starting-points in their own right) is labelled *Action*, *Composition*, *Discussion* and *Research* to indicate the emphasis of the activities envisaged—but, again as in 'People', in these volumes one use of English develops out of and flows into the next.

In Stage One the emphasis lies on the pupil's exploration, through his senses and imagination, of the physical world around him and the inner world of fantasy; while in Stage Two these elements are developed to include the animal world and man's relation to it, leading in Stage 3 to a study of heroes that in turn causes the pupil to examine his own emotions in a series of dramatic situations that prepares him for the issues raised in 'People'.

These books, then, should be seen as starting-points for the individual teacher's own exploration of the themes raised in them. There is a reading-list at the end of the books which will extend the range of their reference, most of them available in paperback, thus perhaps finding their way into the pupil's own library. Some books used here as the basis for extracts may in themselves become the subjects of closer study through the work suggested here, either in their subject-matter or in themselves as literature: for instance, 'Beowulf', 'Shane', 'Tom-Sawyer'/'Huckleberry Finn', 'The Silver Sword' and 'Dawn Wind' are used in my Department for close study and as the basis for extensive imaginative work in writing and drama with pupils of 13 +, and the Greek and Norse Legends, the Alan Garner novels, and 'The Hobbit' and 'The Lord of the Rings' similarly with the 11 to 12s. All the material here has been thoroughly tested in the classroom, forming the basis of a team-teaching syllabus in my Department.

Further poems and photographs will be found in my anthology, 'Dragonsteeth', whose themes connect closely with and extend the range of those explored in 'The Quest'.

Contents

1 Meeting point

A You are here

Discussion

Discuss the differences between life at your previous school and the one you attend now. If you have come from different schools, compare them. What do you miss most in your previous school? What worries you about your new one? What do you like about it?

Read the following story by William Saroyan.

He was a little boy named Jim, the first and only child of Dr. Louis Davy, 717 Mattei Building, and it was his first day at school. His father was French, a small heavy-set man of forty whose boyhood had been full of poverty and unhappiness and ambition. His mother was dead: she died when Jim was born, and the only woman he knew intimately was Amy, the Swedish housekeeper.

It was Amy who dressed him in his Sunday clothes and took him to school. Jim liked Amy, but he didn't like her for taking him to school. He told her so. All the way to school, he told her so.

'I don't like you,' he said. 'I don't like you any more.'

'I like *you*,' the housekeeper said.

'Then why are you taking me to school?' he said.

He had taken walks with Amy before, once all the way to the Court House Park for the Sunday afternoon band concert, but this walk to school was different.

'What for?' he said.

'Everybody must go to school,' the housekeeper said.

'Did you go to school?' he said.

1

'No,' said Amy.

'Then why do I have to go?' he said.

'You will like it,' said the housekeeper.

He walked on with her in silence, holding her hand. 'I don't like you,' he said. 'I don't like you any more.'

'I like you,' said Amy.

'Then why are you taking me to school?' he said again. 'Why?'

The housekeeper knew how frightened a little boy could be about going to school.

'You will like it,' she said. 'I think you will sing songs and play games.'

'I don't want to,' he said.

'I will come and get you every afternoon,' she said.

'I don't like you,' he told her again.

She felt very unhappy about the little boy going to school, but she knew that he would have to go.

The school building was very ugly to her and to the boy. She didn't like the way it made her feel, and going up the steps with him she wished he didn't have to go to school. The halls and rooms scared her, and him, and the smell of the place too. And she didn't like Mr. Barber, the principal.

Amy despised Mr. Barber.

'What is the name of your son?' Mr. Barber said.

'This is Dr. Louis Davy's son,' said Amy. 'His name is Jim. I am Dr. Davy's housekeeper.'

'James?' said Mr. Barber.

'Not James,' said Amy, 'just Jim.'

'All right,' said Mr. Barber. 'Any middle name?'

'No,' said Amy. 'He is too small for a middle name. Just Jim Davy.'

'All right,' said Mr. Barber. 'We'll try him out in the first grade. If he doesn't get along all right we'll try him out in kindergarten.'

'Dr. Davy said to start him in the first grade,' said Amy. 'Not kindergarten.'

'All right,' said Mr. Barber.

The housekeeper knew how frightened the little boy was, sitting on the chair, and she tried to let him know how much she loved him and how sorry she was about everything, but she couldn't say anything, and she was very proud of the nice way he got down from the chair and stood beside Mr. Barber, waiting to go with him to a classroom.

On the way home she was so proud of him she began to cry.

Miss Binney, the teacher of the first grade, was an old lady who was all dried out. The room was full of little boys and girls. School smelled strange and sad. He sat at a desk and listened carefully.

He heard some of the names: Charles, Ernest, Alvin, Norman, Betty, Hannah, Juliet, Viola, Polly.

He listened carefully and heard Miss Binney say, 'Hannah Winter, what *are* you chewing?' And he saw Hannah Winter blush. He liked Hannah Winter right from the beginning.

'Gum,' said Hannah.

'Put it in the waste-basket,' said Miss Binney.

He saw the little girl walk to the front of the class, take the gum from her mouth, and drop it into the waste-basket.

And he heard Miss Binney say, 'Ernest Gaskin, what are *you* chewing?'

'Gum,' said Ernest.

And he liked Ernest Gaskin too.

They met in the schoolyard, and Ernest taught him a few jokes.

Amy was in the hall when school ended. She was sullen and angry at everybody until she saw the little boy. She was amazed that he wasn't changed, that he wasn't hurt, or perhaps utterly unalive, murdered. The school and everything about it frightened her very much. She took his hand and walked out of the building with him, feeling angry and proud.

Jim said, 'What comes after twenty-nine?'

'Thirty,' said Amy.

'Your face is dirty,' he said.

His father was very quiet at the supper table.

'What comes after twenty-nine?' the boy said.

'Thirty,' said his father.

'Your face is dirty,' he said.

In the morning he asked his father for a nickel.

'What do you want a nickel for?' his father said.

'Gum,' he said.

His father gave him a nickel and on the way to school he

stopped at Mrs. Riley's store and bought a package of Spearmint.

'Do you want a piece?' he asked Amy.

'Do you want to give me a piece?' the housekeeper said.

Jim thought about it a moment, and then he said, 'Yes.'

'Do you like me?' said the housekeeper.

'I like you,' said Jim. 'Do you like me?'

'Yes,' said the housekeeper.

'Do you like school?'

Jim didn't know for sure, but he knew he liked the part about the gum. And Hannah Winter. And Ernest Gaskin.

'I don't know,' he said.

'Do you sing?' asked the housekeeper.

'No, we don't sing,' he said.

'Do you play games?' she said.

'Not in the school,' he said. 'In the yard we do.'

He liked the part about gum very much.

Miss Binney said, 'Jim Davy, what are you *chewing*?'

'Ha ha ha,' he thought.

'Gum,' he said.

He walked to the waste-paper basket and back to his seat, and Hannah Winter saw him, and Ernest Gaskin too. That was the best part of school.

It began to grow too.

'Ernest Gaskin,' he shouted in the schoolyard, '*what* are you *chewing*?'

'Raw elephant meat,' said Ernest Gaskin. 'Jim Davy, what are *you* chewing?'

Jim tried to think of something very funny to be chewing, but he couldn't.

'Gum,' he said, and Ernest Gaskin laughed louder than Jim laughed when Ernest Gaskin said raw elephant meat.

It was funny no matter what you said.

Going back to the classroom Jim saw Hannah Winter in the hall.

'Hannah Winter,' he said, '*what in the world* are you *chewing*?'

The little girl was startled. She wanted to say something nice that would honestly show how nice she felt about having Jim say her name and ask her the funny question, making fun of

4

school, but she couldn't think of anything that nice to say because they were almost in the room and there wasn't time enough.

'Tutti-frutti,' she said with desperate haste.

It seemed to Jim he had never before heard such a glorious word, and he kept repeating the word to himself all day.

'Tutti-frutti,' he said to Amy on the way home.

'Amy Larson,' he said, *what, are, you, chewing?*'

He told his father all about it at the supper table.

He said, 'Once there was a hill. On the hill there was a mill. Under the mill there was a walk. Under the walk there was a key. What is it?'

'I don't know,' his father said. 'What is it?'

'Milwaukee,' said the boy.

The housekeeper was delighted.

'Mill. Walk. Key,' Jim said.

Tutti-frutti.

'What's that?' said his father.

'Gum,' he said. 'The kind Hannah Winter chews.'

'Who's Hannah Winter?' said his father.

'She's in my room,' he said.

'Oh,' said his father.

After supper he sat on the floor with the small red and blue and yellow top that hummed while it spinned. It was all right, he guessed. It was still very sad, but the gum part of it was very funny and the Hannah Winter part very nice. Raw elephant meat, he thought with great inward delight.

'Raw elephant meat,' he said aloud to his father who was reading the evening paper. His father folded the paper and sat on the floor beside him.

The housekeeper saw them together on the floor and for some reason tears came to her eyes.

Why do you think tears came into the eyes of the housekeeper at the end? How does she feel about Jim going to school? How does Jim's attitude towards school change? What is 'the best part of school' for him? Why does he keep repeating words he hears? Was it the same for you when you started your first school?

Tell one another about your experiences there. What frightened you? How did you overcome that fear? What did you find difficult? Discuss the teachers you had, and the amusing experiences that befell you. Perhaps someone in the group started school in a different part of the country from where you live—if so, you can compare the similarities and differences in your first schools. Have you been back to your infant school recently? If so, how did it strike you on your return compared with when you first saw it?

Action

1 In groups of four, work out a simple clapping rhythm that will be easy to remember. Practise it together, until you are sure of it. Decide which pair is going to clap and which will listen.

2 Now divide into these pairs, and join with the other pairs in the class to form two lines facing one another at opposite ends of the room: one line will be made up of those pairs who are going to clap and the other line of those who are going to listen.

3 The line of pairs listening close your eyes and wait till you hear your rhythm being clapped. When you are sure of it, join in and clap in time with the other pair in your group. Keep your eyes closed: you have only your ears to guide you, and will find it increasingly difficult to concentrate.

4 The line of pairs who are going to clap wait for a signal from your teacher to start clapping. One pair will start and when its partners at the other end of the room have joined in, another pair will be brought in, and so on, until all the groups are clapping simultaneously: you will thus find it increasingly difficult to get your messages across to the pairs at the other end of the room.

5 Now reverse the procedure, so that the pairs who started the clapping find out for themselves how difficult it is to join in. Were there too many rhythms being clapped at the same time on the first trial? If so, perhaps half the class will try at a time. Were some of the rhythms too similar? If so, it will be necessary to change them.

Read the following suggestions carefully and then join with the other groups to form one large ring.

6 Stand apart from everyone else in a space where there is room to move about. Close your eyes and keep still, then listen to all the noises happening in the school around you. Really concentrate, so that you are aware of *every* sound, even the sound of your own breathing.

7 When told to do so by your teacher, change your focus of concentration. Think now about yourself, your own body. With your eyes closed, focus your attention on one part of your body: be aware of it as you have never been before, so that you forget about every one else in the room and about everything except this one focal point that demands every part of your attention, like a pain nagging at you.

8 Now concentrate on your feet. Wiggle your toes with your feet placed firmly on the floor. Now move your ankles, still without moving from where you are standing, then toes and ankles. Gradually add more actions to those you have started: first your legs, then fingers and hands, arms, head, mouth and jaws, eyes and eyebrows—until you are moving every part of your body.

9 Stand still. Fix your eyes on another part of the room. When told to, move towards that part *without touching anyone*, and when you get there stop.

10 Now choose another part of the room and do exactly the

same. This time when you get there change direction without stopping and move to another part, staring fixedly ahead of you all the time. Keep on doing this until told to stop, gradually walking more quickly, but without touching anyone.

11 Think about the surface of the floor you are walking on. At a given signal the ground beneath your feet changes to **a** sand **b** tar **c** glass **d** ice **e** water.
Let the way you move show what has happened to the ground beneath you.

12 Sit down. Feel the real floor you have been walking on. Tell yourself what messages the nerves in your fingers are

sending to your brain. Now find a rough surface for them to touch. Place one hand on the smooth surface of the floor and the other on the rough surface you have chosen. Now focus all your attention first on the smooth surface, then on the rough surface, and finally on the smooth again. Concentrate wholly on this, as you did before.

13 Now look closely at your fingers. Your fingers are unique. They can't be matched by any others in the world. Study them. Make them into puppets: let them show
a fear **b** anger **c** old age **d** tiredness **e** joy.

14 Look at your fingertips. Study your fingerprint. Trace the unique pattern the lines form.

15 Now use your fingers to take your pulse. Lie down and feel the rhythm of your breathing, hear the beating of your heart. Feel your blood moving around your veins.

Composition

1 Close your eyes again and sit still so that you can hear all the sounds around you and outside the building.
Write down quickly the exact words to describe what you have heard, then discuss what you have noted down, comparing one another's versions of the same sound to find the most accurate ways of describing it—have you used words that in themselves make a lot of sound when spoken or even imitate the sound they describe, words like hum, grunt, shout, sing, whinny, moo, caw, whistle, hiss, squeak, slam, rustle, whisper? When you have decided on the right words, make a careful description of the sounds you have heard.

2 Look outside and study the view through the window: notice the colours, textures and shapes of the buildings; of the shadows they form; the movement of the wind in grass and twig; the shapes and movements of trees and clouds;

the changing light in the sky and its effects on the scene around you. Make brief notes again of what you see. Use comparisons with other things that will help someone to visualize what you are seeing now even though he won't

have been with you at the time of writing—like these written by Laurie Lee:

'Streams ran from holes, and back into holes, like noisy underground trains.'

'The tiles grew a kind of golden moss which sparkled like crystallized honey.'

'There were jigsaws of frost on the window.'

'A fountain of sparks shot high into the night, writhing and sweeping on the wind, falling and dancing along the road.

The chimney hissed like a firework, great rockets of flame came gushing forth. . . .'

'I had never been so close to grass before. It towered above me and all around me, each blade tattooed with tiger-skins of sunlight. It was knife-edged, dark, and a wicked green, thick as a forest and alive with grasshoppers that chirped and chattered and leapt through the air like monkeys.'

Again, discuss your notes and then build them into a careful description.

3 Now go outside and smell the air: feel its pressure on your cheek as you move, and notice the effect of the change of temperature on your body. Return slowly into the classroom, noticing the way the sounds of your voices and feet change as you go inside, the change in the light, the ways in which people's appearances change, the different sounds and smells in the classroom itself. Look back at your last paragraph and compare your sensations then with those you felt outside. Make notes on all these things, and then build them into a final paragraph. Use the comparison I mentioned in the last but one sentence to link your present paragraph with those you have written already.

4 Use one of the photographs that illustrate this section as the basis for a poem on the same subject, or on the thoughts and feelings that the picture arouses in you. Again, note down briefly the points you want to make, then use them as the starting-points for lines: don't concern yourself with rhymes (unless they fall into place naturally) and let the order and pattern of your poem grow as your thoughts take shape. Remember to use comparisons as you have done above, and again concentrate on the way these pictures (or the images that come to your mind) affect your senses.

5 In the group of four you were in for the Action section above, make up a group poem for you to speak to the rest

of the class. The subject of your poem is the School Canteen or Dining Hall:

a Make notes individually first under the headings of the senses, choosing the most distinctive sights, sounds, smells, etc., and trying to describe them vividly and powerfully, but as briefly as possible too.

b The four of you pool your ideas and choose the best ones, arranging them in the most effective order—perhaps other, better ideas will arise in the discussion as well.

c Next arrange the lines for speaking, deciding which are best spoken individually and which by more than one person, to give variety to your performance.

d Can you make sounds that will help to underline what your poem says? If so, add them.

e Rehearse your poems thoroughly, then perform them to the rest of the class.

Action

1 Try to imagine what it must be like to be blind. Read carefully the following sequence of actions and, when you think you can remember them all, perform them with your eyes firmly closed.

a Find your pen or pencil and exercise book, then put them on the desk before you.

b Write today's date on the top line of a clean page.

c Find the thickest and thinnest objects in your case or satchel and put them on the desk.

d Get up and change places with whoever is sitting nearest you.

e Give each other the objects on the desk before you, together with your cases or satchels, then put your books back exactly where you found them.

2 Discuss with your partner how you can make that sequence of actions more difficult. For instance, your pencil may

need sharpening first; when your eyes are closed, your satchel may be placed by someone else within reach of where you are sitting but not where you left it, etc.

Now perform the modified actions again.

3 Number yourselves One and Two. Number One is blind: Number Two has to guide him, by word alone, from one end of the classroom to his desk.

Now change over and let Number One guide Number Two in the same way.

4 Number One: you have sprained your ankle. You are lying in the middle of the road. Number Two: you are blind and hear Number One's cry of pain, so try to reach him to offer help.

Number One: direct Number Two towards you, bearing in mind the obstacles that he may trip over or fall into on the way unless your instructions are very clear.

Again, change roles as you did in 3.

5 With the rest of the class sitting with eyes closed, one person moves around the classroom performing ten actions, each with a distinctive sound (e.g. switching on the lights, opening a desk, writing on the blackboard). When you have finished, test the class's memory.

Discussion

1 Discuss what you learned about your senses in the Action section above. What was the effect on your other senses of losing your sight?

Each pair join with another pair to form a group. Now:

2 Tell one another of any experience you may have had of meeting, watching or helping a blind person. Did you notice then any of the effects you discussed in 1?

3 Discuss whether you think it would be worse to have been born blind or deaf, explaining your reasons.

4 Test whether your sight is lazy: in each pair, Number One close your eyes while Number Two asks you questions about what can be seen in the room around you, and the view from the window. Then change over, as before.

5 Sit back to back and try to describe one another.

Research

1 Read the story of Helen Keller and tell the rest of the class what you learn about her, describing what you think must have been the most memorable event in her life.

2 At home (and observed by someone else to prevent accidents!) try some simple domestic tasks without the aid of your sight. Write about what happened, and at school tell the rest of the class what happened to you.

3 Find out about guide dogs, and how they are trained, then give a talk about their life and work.

4 Do you know of anyone who has triumphed over his physical handicap (not necessarily blindness) and perhaps been an example through his courage and endurance for others to follow? If so, find out more about this person for a talk to the rest of the class.

5 Discuss what help physically handicapped people need, having found out as much as you can about what is being done for them already. Can more be done? What can you yourselves do?

B Summer

Action

1 Walk about the room without touching anyone (as you did in Section A).
2 Imagine yourself to be someone else: think of someone you know well and practise walking around as he would—a small prop like a hat, a newspaper, a pair of gloves or spectacles may help you get into the 'feel' of your character.
3 You (your character) are waiting at a busy railway station. You are anxious. Perhaps the train is late? Perhaps something important has to be done when you reach the end of your journey? Or perhaps you are waiting eagerly for the arrival of someone whom you expect to be on this train? Think out *your* reason for being anxious. Notice how it affects your movements.
4 Get into groups of four to six. You are a family going on holiday at the peak of the summer holiday season. Work out the characters, then discuss the anxieties that they will have. Work out your scene, then show it to another group.

5 Both groups now work out a scene that involves the two families meeting. Start from your separate scenes as you worked them out in **4** and let them grow into one involving all of you. What is going to cause your coming together? Perhaps an unruly child annoys someone in the other family, causing an argument? Perhaps the families know one another already but haven't met for a long time? Perhaps a small child gets lost and finds himself in the other family? Are both families travelling to the same destination?

6 Act all the scenes simultaneously, but as a class add the following:
   a a bookseller at the station bookstall
   b a policeman
   c two porters
   d two buffet attendants
   e a ticket collector

The presence of these will change your scenes: if other things happen because of being with the other groups, follow them up and see what results.

7 Discuss what happened in **6**. Was enough use made of the new characters? Are the 'officials' needed? Were there some good ideas that weren't developed fully or didn't work out properly? Criticize the weaknesses of your scene and suggest what could be done to improve them.

8 Now put your improvements into practice, adding the factor that the train is half an hour late.

9 Discuss how a story could emerge from the scene you have built, especially when the train arrives. More changes in the 'cast' may be necessary. At the moment there are only families (besides the extra characters listed in **6**): perhaps one group could change its characters? Use one of these suggestions as a starting-point:
   a a TV personality is seen among the crowd
   b a heavily-guarded criminal boards the train
   c someone falls onto the line as the train approaches the platform
   d there is a pickpocket in the crowd: someone has been

robbed of a lot of money and accuses an innocent by-
stander (perhaps, for instance, one of the children in a
family, or a tramp)

  e the station-manager is new and manages to cause great
  confusion.

10 Work out your story, not forgetting to make the scene as
real as you did in **8**. Start by re-enacting what happened
then, and let the story grow from there.

Composition

1 Write the story that you acted above from the point of view
of your character.
2 Make a story from the photographs that illustrate this
section. Again tell it from the point of view of a character—
the child, the policeman, the child's mother, the Station
Inspector, or your own character again, watching from
nearby.

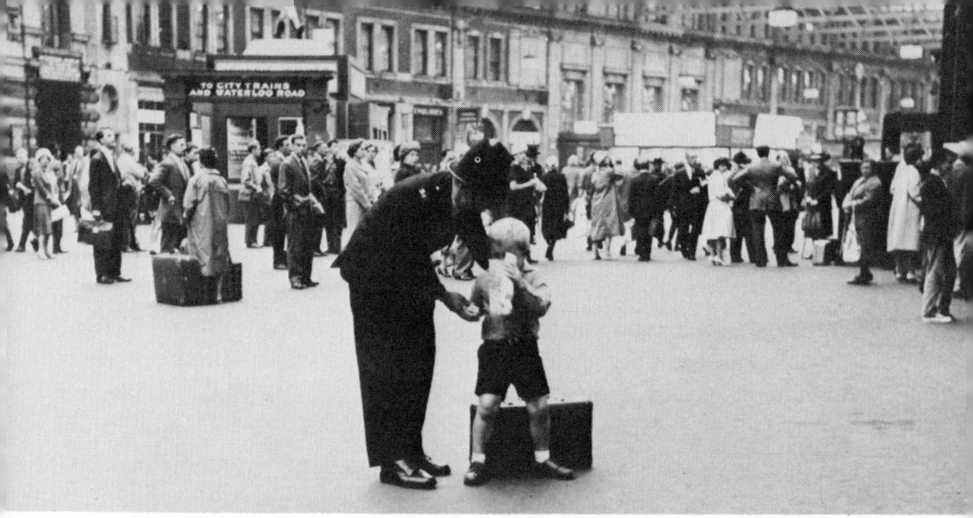
TO CITY TRAINS
AND WATERLOO ROAD

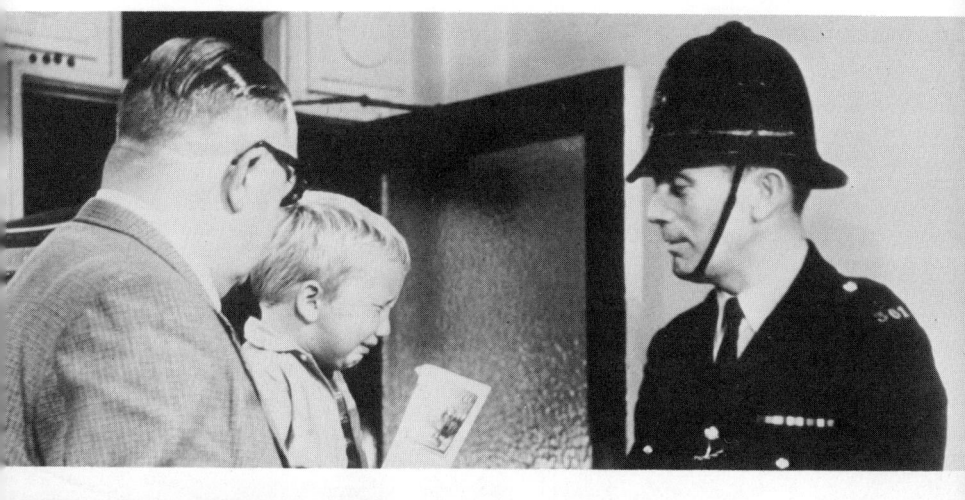

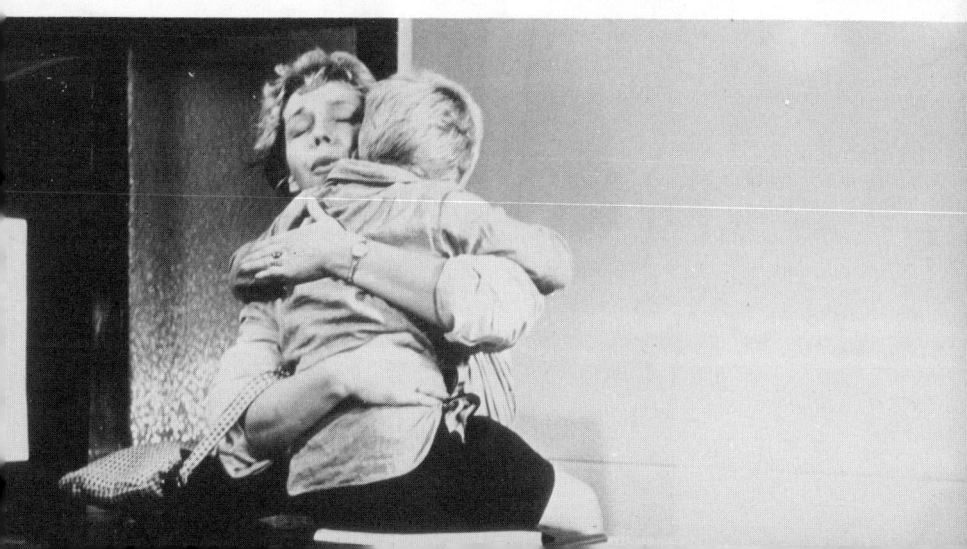

3 A small toy on a seat reminds a porter of a little boy he saw in tears half an hour ago . . . Describe what happens.
4 Write your own most memorable story of when you found yourself lost in a strange but crowded place, with no parent to look after you.
5 Describe either an event that happened to you in a busy terminus (not necessarily a railway station—perhaps a bus station, an airport, or a harbour) that you want the class to know about, or the preparations and start of a holiday (not the holiday itself) that you will always remember—perhaps because everything went wrong.

Discussion

1 Use the stories you wrote in 5 above as the basis for talks to the class or group about a memorable holiday.
2 Discuss which ways of spending a holiday are the most enjoyable.

3 What do you look forward to most as the summer holidays approach at the end of a long term? Do your holidays always match up to your expectations of them? Do you feel the same about them after a month as you did at the beginning? Describe how your feelings change as the holidays progress and term approaches — think back to this last holiday and tell the group how you spent it and how you felt about it.

4 Read the following story and then discuss what Julia feels about the trout. Why does the writer say at the end: 'Like a river of joy her holiday spread before her'?

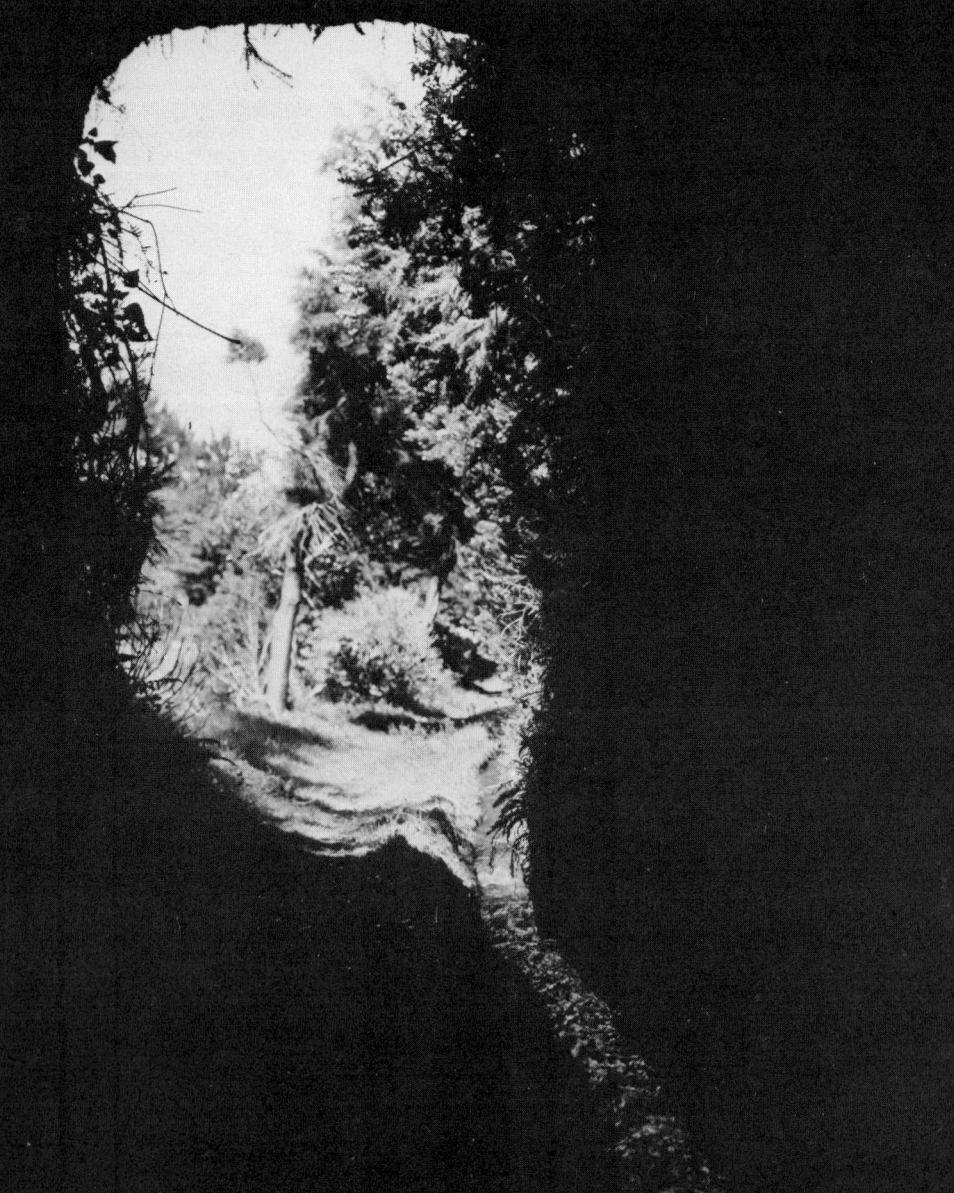

One of the first places Julia always ran to when they arrived was the Dark Walk. It is a laurel walk, very old; almost gone wild, a lofty midnight tunnel of smooth, sinewy branches. Underfoot the tough brown leaves are never dry enough to crackle: there is always a suggestion of damp and cool trickle.

She raced right into it. For the first few yards she always had the memory of the sun behind her, then she felt the dusk closing swiftly down on her so that she screamed with pleasure and raced on to reach the light at the far end; and it was always just a little too long in coming so that she emerged gasping, clasping her hands, laughing, drinking in the sun. When she was filled with the heat and glare she would turn and consider the ordeal again.

This year she had the extra joy of showing it to her small brother, and of terrifying him as well as herself. And for him the fear lasted longer because his legs were so short and she had gone out at the far end while he was still screaming and racing.

When they had done this many times they came back to the house to tell everybody that they had done it. He boasted. She mocked. They squabbled.

'Cry baby!'

'You were afraid yourself, so there!'

'I won't take you any more.'

'You're a big pig.'

'I hate you.'

Tears were threatening so somebody said, 'Did you see the well?' She opened her eyes at that and held up her long lovely neck suspiciously and decided to be incredulous. She was twelve and at that age girls are beginning to suspect more stories. They have already found out too many, from Santa Claus to the stork. How could there be a well? In the Dark Walk? That she had visited year after year? Haughtily, she said, 'Nonsense.'

But she went back, pretending to go somewhere else, and she found a hole scooped in the rock at the side of the walk, choked with damp leaves, so shrouded by ferns that she uncovered it only after much searching. At the back of this little cavern there was about a quart of water. In the water she suddenly perceived a panting trout. She rushed for Stephen and dragged him to see, and they were both so excited that they were no longer afraid of the darkness as they hunched down and peered in at the fish panting in his tiny prison, his silver stomach going up and down like an engine.

Nobody knew how the trout got there. Even old Martin in the kitchen garden laughed and refused to believe that it was there, or pretended not to believe, until she forced him to come down and see. Kneeling and pushing back his tattered old cap he peered in.

'Be cripes, you're right. How the divil in hell did that fella get there?'

She stared at him suspiciously.

'You knew?' she accused: but he said, 'The divil a' know,' and reached down to lift it out. Convinced she hauled him back. If she had found it, then it was her trout.

Her mother suggested that a bird had carried the spawn. Her father thought that in the winter a small streamlet might have carried it down there as a baby, and it had been safe until the summer came and the water began to dry up. She said, 'I see,' and went back to look again and consider the matter in private. Her brother remained behind, waiting to hear the whole story of the trout, not really interested in the actual trout but much interested in the story which his mummy began to make up for him on the lines of 'So one day Daddy Trout and Mummy Trout . . .' When he retailed it to her, she said, 'Pooh.'

It troubled her that the trout was always in the same position; he had no room to turn; all the time the silver belly went up and down; otherwise he was motionless. She wondered what he ate, and in between visits to Joey Pony and the boat and a bathe to get cool, she thought of his hunger. She brought him a worm. He ignored the food. He just went on panting. Hunched over him she thought how all the winter, while she was at the school, he had been in there. All the winter, in the Dark Walk, all day, all night, floating around alone. She drew the leaf of her hat down around her ears and chin and stared. She was still thinking of it as she lay in bed.

It was late June, the longest days of the year. The sun had sat still for a week, burning up the world. Although it was after ten o'clock it was still bright and still hot. She lay on her back under a single sheet, with her long legs spread, trying to keep cool. She could see the D of the moon through the fir tree —

26

they slept on the ground floor. Before they went to bed her mummy had told Stephen the story of the trout again, and she, in her bed, had resolutely presented her back to them and read her book. But she had kept one ear cocked.

'And so in the end, this naughty fish who would not stay at home got bigger and bigger and bigger, and the water got smaller and smaller. . . .'

Passionately she had whirled and cried, 'Mummy, don't make it a horrible old moral story!' Her mummy had brought in a fairy godmother then, who sent lots of rain, and filled the well, and a stream poured out and the trout floated away down to the river below. Staring at the moon she knew that there are no such things as fairy godmothers and that the trout, down in the Dark Walk, was panting, like an engine. She heard somebody unwind a fishing reel. Would the *beasts* fish him out?

She sat up. Stephen was a hot lump of sleep, lazy thing. The Dark Walk would be full of little scraps of moon. She leaped up and looked out the window, and somehow it was not so lightsome now that she saw the dim mountains far away and the black firs against the breathing land and heard a dog say *bark-bark*. Quietly she lifted the ewer of water and climbed out the window and scuttled along the cool but cruel gravel down to the maw of her tunnel. Her pyjamas were very short so that when she splashed water it wet her ankles. She peered into the tunnel. Something alive rustled inside there. She raced in, and up and down she raced, and flurried, and cried aloud, 'Oh gosh, I can't find it,' and then at last she did. Kneeling down in the damp she put her hand into the slimy hole. When the body lashed they were both mad with fright. But she gripped him and shoved him into the ewer and raced, with her teeth ground, out to the other end of the tunnel and down the steep paths to the river's edge.

All the time she could feel him lashing his tail against the side of the ewer. She was afraid he would jump right out. The gravel cut into her soles until she came to the cool ooze of the river's bank where the moon mice on the water crept into her feet. She poured out, watching until he plopped. For a second he was visible in the water. She hoped he was not dizzy. Then all she saw was the glimmer of the moon in the silent-flowing river, the dark firs, the dim mountains, and the radiant pointed face laughing down at her out of the empty sky.

She scuttled up the hill, in the window, plonked down the ewer, and flew through the air like a bird into bed. The dog said *bark-bark*. She heard the fishing reel whirring. She hugged herself and giggled. Like a river of joy her holiday spread before her.

In the morning Stephen rushed to her, shouting that 'he' was gone, and asking 'where' and 'how'. Lifting her nose in the air she said superciliously, 'Fairy godmother, I suppose?' and strolled away, patting the palms of her hands.

Sean O'Faolain

Why does Julia answer Stephen 'superciliously' here? Discuss her attitude towards 'stories' — why is she suspicious of them? Would you call her an unimaginative person? Quote examples from the story above to prove what you think.

Perhaps this story reminds you of a similar conflict with your family or of a time when you gave a wild animal its freedom? If so, tell the group about it.

5 Now read the following poem by Norman MacCaig, and discuss the mood it creates:

Summer Farm

Straws like tame lightnings lie about the grass
And hang zigzag on hedges. Green as glass
The water in the horse-trough shines.
Nine ducks go wobbling by in two straight lines.

A hen stares at nothing with one eye,
Then picks it up. Out of an empty sky
A swallow falls and, flickering through
The barn, dives up again into the dizzy blue.

I lie, not thinking, in the cool, soft grass.
Afraid of where a thought might take me — as
This grasshopper with plated face
Unfolds his legs and finds himself in space.

Self under self, a pile of selves I stand
Threaded on time, and with metaphysic hand
Lift the farm like a lid and see
Farm within farm, and in the centre, me.

Norman MacCaig

C Harvest

Composition

Read the poem above and the descriptions of summer you can
find in the story by Sean O'Faolain, then:
1 Write about (perhaps in a poem, as above) a hot day this
   summer when everything was heavy and still: try to recap-
   ture the atmosphere and your feelings in your writing.
2 Read closely the end of the story — when Julia gets up at
   night and releases the fish. Think about why the writer included these words and phrases:
   'the breathing land'
   'the cool but cruel gravel'
   'with her teeth ground'

'the moon mice on the water crept into her feet'
'the radiant pointed face laughing down at her out of the empty sky'
What do they add to the meaning and atmosphere of the scene?
Now write about a hot summer's night when you could not sleep, but had to get up and go outside; or about a still night that developed into a storm.

3 Look carefully at one of the pictures of the sea in this section. Use one of them as an illustration to a poem, in the same way as I have. The photograph facing reminds me of a particular beach in Pembrokeshire, and what I thought about the cliffs there:

Brazen stumps of arms thrusting
Scars at the sea's bite: but
Defiant lines scowled in salt
Cannot outface, for

            behind them
Press a leering gallery of gargoyles
Waiting for the sea's callous lick to
Pommel those frowns into sandcastles

Your poem may also be about how the summer calm changes, bringing with it a sense of danger: perhaps the feeling that soon the holidays will be over, school and winter looming ahead, or how the still calm surface is whipped into a raging storm, or how the same sea that you bathe in and divert into moats for sandcastles has drowned people and caused villages to collapse.

Research

1 Find out about occasions when the sea has caused devastation through flooding, in fact and in legend. Tell the class about them.

2 The sea is also a great source of wealth to man: find out about its treasures for a talk called 'The Harvest of the Seas'.

3 Discuss how the earth creates and destroys life for man, in the same way as you have discussed the sea.

4 Describe to the rest of your group or class Harvest Festival in your church and your feelings about it.

5 About two thirds of the world's population are starving. Find out about their plight and how it is caused. What is being done for them? What else should be done? Put your thoughts into words that can be used for a special Harvest Festival service that looks at both sides of the coin — the cause for rejoicing and the cause for concern.

2 Change

A Autumn and winter

The Sheaf

I'd often seen before
That sheaf of corn hung from the bough—
Strange in a wood a sheaf of corn
Though by the woods half torn
And thrashed by rain to empty straw.
And then to-day I saw
A small pink twitching snout
And eyes like black beads sewn in fur
Peep from a hole in doubt,
And heard on dry leaves go tat-tat
The stiff tail of the other rat.
And now as the short day grows dim
And here and there farms in the dark
Turn to spark,
I on my stumbling way think how
With indistinguishable limb
And tight tail round each other's head
They'll make to-night one ball in bed,
Those long-tailed lovers who have come
To share the pheasants' harvest-home.

Andrew Young

Research

In groups, study and chart the changing of autumn into winter, writing reports for a classroom exhibition, illustrated by drawings, collages and objects you have collected. Each group take one of the following categories:

a migration   **b** hibernation   **c** trees   **d** weather   **e** people.

Here are some suggestions of what each group may do: you will add more yourselves in discussion.

1 Classify the birds in your area that you know will be migrating this autumn. Observe their preparations and record the dates on which they leave. Find out from library books where they are going and what will happen to them in the future, and about other birds that leave this country for the winter.

2 Decide which animals you can observe and study them individually, noticing carefully how they prepare for the winter, how their fur thickens and changes, etc. Include pets, like tortoises, as well as wild animals. Use library

books to find out more details about the animals you are observing and about other animals that you can't observe.

3 Study and draw the changing shapes of various species of trees in your area, and collect and press their freshly-fallen leaves. Collect nuts and berries. Describe your findings as accurately as you can. Talk to gardeners and use gardening books from the library to find out more about the trees you are studying, and about pruning. Describe the falling leaves, particularly on a windy day, scuff through the fallen leaves when wet and when dry, and describe the various sounds your feet make, as well as the different shapes and colours of leaves and twigs. Perhaps your notes can be built into a collage of words to accompany a collage of objects.

4 Observe closely the changing weather as the days grow shorter and colder, and write descriptions of the sky. Choose a scene to describe the various stages of the autumn and describe the effects of the oncoming winter on people's appearance and behaviour. As you observe different weathers describe them accurately by using library books to identify the different types of clouds, etc. Make weather-charts like those used by meteorologists and check on the accuracy of their forecasts—for instance, by collecting cuttings from a week's newspapers and writing reports on what actually happened. Compare the changes in the weather with what is happening in the rest of Europe.

5 Observe how people react to the changes in the weather. Study (from observation or library books) and describe what farmers have to do at this time of the year. Make a study (with drawings and cuttings from newspapers and magazines) of the colours and styles of autumn fashions. Describe the early evenings at various stages of the autumn, focussing on a particular street in your neighbourhood and how the scene changes at, say, 6 p.m.

Decide how the work is going to be divided among the members of the group and carry this work on through October and November for an eventual exhibition.

Action

Read the following poem by Laurie Lee:

Field of Autumn

Slow moves the acid breath of noon
over the copper-coated hill,
slow from the wild crab's bearded breast
the palsied apples fall.

Like coloured smoke the day hangs fire,
taking the village without sound;
the vulture-headed sun lies low
chained to the violet ground.

The horse upon the rocky height
rolls all the valley in his eye,
but dares not raise his foot or move
his shoulder from the fly.

The sheep, snail-backed against the wall,
lifts her blind face but does not know
the cry her blackened tongue gives forth
is the first bleat of snow.

Each bird and stone, each roof and well,
feels the gold foot of autumn pass;
each spider binds with glittering snare
the splintered bones of grass.

Slow moves the hour that sucks our life,
slow drops the late wasp from the pear,
the rose tree's thread of scent draws thin—
and snaps upon the air.

1 Discuss what the poem tells us about autumn and the mood it creates. Pay close attention to the sounds of the poem: how do they help to achieve this mood? Listen similarly to the poem's rhythm.

2 In groups of four to five practise reciting this poem. Divide the lines among you in ways that will underline the shifts in the poem's meaning. Which lines will be said individually and which together or in pairs? Make sure that in dividing up the poem you don't make it sound jerky.

3 Rehearse and then perform the poem to another group. Criticize constructively one another's performances. Is the mood that you defined in 1 made clear in these performances, or are they monotonous and lifeless? Has enough attention been paid to the poem's sounds and rhythm? Give suggestions to one another on how the reciting can be improved.

4 Rehearse the poem again, putting into action the suggestions made to you by the other group. Then perform the poem again, this time to the rest of the class.

5 Make a recording of the best performance of the poem, or of a class performance using the best ideas that have emerged from the work done in groups. Now in the same groups work out a sequence of movements that will go with the words: use simple movements, sometimes working singly and sometimes together, that will help to communicate the mood of the poem that you discussed earlier and tried to convey in your reading of the poem. Again, show them to the rest of the class and then put the best ideas together with the words for a class performance of the poem, combining speech and action.

Composition

Read the following poems by Ronald Duncan:

September

An old gypsy
with last year's apple face
And merry-berry eyes;
A loose shawl
Over her bent shoulders,
wearing slippers of leaves
Shuffles into the farmyard.
She carries lavender
But September is certain to sell you
A bushel of saffron sleep.

October

Like severed hands the wet leaves lie
Flat on the deserted avenue;
Houses like skulls stare through uncurtained windows,
A woman dressed like a furled umbrella
With a zip-fastener on her mouth
Steps out of number fifty-three
To post a letter. Her gloved hand
Hesitates at the box: then knowing there'll be no reply
She tears it up and throws it in the gutter.
And autumn with its pheasant's tail
Consoles her with chrysanthemums.

Notice how the poet has captured the mood of each month in the imagery that he uses. In this respect, what is similar in each poem? How are wet leaves 'like severed hands'? How are houses 'like skulls'?

Write your poems for these months, and add one for November.

Again, choose an image that you can build your poem around, as Ronald Duncan has. Inspiration may come from one of the photographs included in this section; or you may prefer to write separately about them, or about a day in November which for you seems to mark the change from the colours of autumn into the dull, drab, leaden greyness of winter. The best poems from the class could be displayed in the exhibition that grows from your research.

B Night

The day was over and we had used it, running errands or prowling the fields. When evening came we returned to the kitchen, back to its smoky comfort, in from the rapidly cooling air to its wrappings of warmth and cooking. We boys came first, scuffling down the bank, singly, like homing crows. Long tongues of shadows licked the curves of the fields and the trees turned plump and still. I had been off to Painswick to pay the rates, running fast through the long, wet grass, and now I was back, panting hard, the job finished, with hay seeds stuck to my legs. A plate of blue smoke hung above our chimney, flat in the motionless air, and every stone in the path as I ran down home shook my bones with arriving joy.

We chopped wood for the night and carried it in; dry beech sticks as brittle as candy. The baker came down with a basket of bread slung carelessly over his shoulder. Eight quartern loaves, cottage-size, black-crusted, were handed in at the door. A few crisp flakes of pungent crust still clung to his empty basket, so we scooped them up on our spit-wet fingers and laid them upon our tongues. The twilight gathered, the baker shouted goodnight, and whistled his way up the bank. Up in the road his black horse waited, the cart lamps smoking red.

Indoors, our Mother was cooking pancakes, her face aglow from the fire. There was a smell of sharp lemon and salty butter, and a burning hiss of oil. The kitchen was dark and convulsive with shadows, no lights had yet been lit. Flames leapt, subsided, corners woke and died, fires burned in a thousand brasses.

'Poke around for the matches, dear boy,' said Mother. 'Damn me if I know where they got to.'

We lit the candles and set them about, each in its proper order: two on the mantelpiece, one on the piano, and one on a plate in the window. Each candle suspended a ball of light, a luminous fragile glow, which swelled and contracted to the spluttering wick or leaned to the moving air. Their flames pushed weakly against the red of the fire, too tenuous to make much headway, revealing our faces more by casts of darkness than by any clear light they threw.

Next we filled and lit the tall iron lamp and placed it on the table. When the wick had warmed and was drawing properly, we turned it up full strength. The flame in the funnel then sprang alive and rose like a pointed flower, began to sing and shudder and grow more radiant, throwing pools of light on the ceiling. Even so, the kitchen remained mostly in shadow, its walls a voluptuous gloom.

The time had come for my violin practice. I began twanging the strings with relish. Mother was still frying and rolling up

pancakes; my brothers lowered their heads and sighed. I
propped my music on the mantelpiece and sliced through a
Russian Dance while sweet smells of resin mixed with lemon
and fat as the dust flew in clouds from my bow. Now and then
I got a note just right, and then Mother would throw me a
glance. A glance of piercing, anxious encouragement as she
side-stepped my swinging arm. Plump in her slippers, one hand
to her cheek, her pan beating time in the other, her hair falling
down about her ears, mouth working to help out the tune—old
and tired though she was, her eyes were a girl's, and it was for
looks such as these that I played.

44

'Splendid!' she cried. 'Top-hole! Clap-clap! Now give us another, me lad.'

So I slashed away at 'William Tell', and when I did that, plates jumped; and Mother skipped gaily around the hearthrug, and even Tony rocked a bit in his chair.

Meanwhile Jack had cleared some boots from the table and started his inscrutable homework. Tony, in his corner, began to talk to the cat and play with some fragments of cloth. So with the curtains drawn close and the pancakes coming, we settled down to the evening. When the kettle boiled and the toast was made, we gathered and had our tea. We grabbed and dodged and passed and snatched, and packed our mouths like pelicans.

Mother ate always standing up, tearing crusts off the loaf with her fingers, a hand-to-mouth feeding that expressed her vigilance, like that of a wireless-operator at sea. For most of Mother's attention was fixed on the grate, whose fire must never go out. When it threatened to do so she became seized with hysteria, wailing and wringing her hands, pouring on oil and chopping up chairs in a frenzy to keep it alive. In fact it seldom went out completely, though it was very often ill. But Mother nursed it with skill, banking it up every night and blowing hard on the bars every morning. The state of our fire became as important to us as it must have been to a primitive tribe. When it sulked and sank we were filled with dismay; when it blazed all was well with the world; but if—God save us—it went out altogether, then we were clutched by primeval chills. Then it seemed that the very sun had died, that winter had come forever, that the wolves of the wilderness were gathering near, and that there was no more hope to look for. . . .

But tonight the firelight snapped and crackled, and Mother was in full control. She ruled the range and all its equipment with a tireless, nervous touch. Eating with one hand, she threw on wood with the other, raked the ashes, and heated the oven, put on a kettle, stirred the pot, and spread out some more shirts on the guard. As soon as we boys had finished our tea, we pushed all the crockery aside, piled it up roughly at the far end of the table, and settled down under the lamp. Its light was warm and live around us, a kind of puddle of fire of its own. I set up my book and began to draw. Jack worked at his notes and figures. Tony was playing with some cotton reels, pushing them slowly round the table.

All was silent except Tony's voice, softly muttering his cotton reel story. '. . . So they come out of this big hole see, and the big chap say Fie and said we'll kill 'em see, and the pirates was waiting up 'ere, and they had this gurt cannon and they went bang fire and the big chap fell down wheeee! and rolled back in the 'ole and I said we got 'em and I run up the 'ill and this boat see was comin' and I jumped on board woosh cruump 'atchet 'ack 'ack and they all fell plop in the sea wallop and I sailed the boat round 'ere and round 'ere and up 'ere and round 'ere and down 'ere and up 'ere and round 'ere and down 'ere . . .'

Laurie Lee, *Cider With Rosie*

Discussion

1 Discuss what Laurie Lee liked about his home in the evenings. What gave him most pleasure? What did he fear?

2 Look carefully at the writer's comparisons in this extract, and discuss the ones you like best: what do they add to the passage? Try to imagine what the effect would be if they were removed.

3 Look especially at the way the writer describes dark things. Why do the shadows have 'tongues'? Why is smoke called a 'plate'? Why are the shadows in the kitchen called 'convulsive'? What does Laurie Lee notice particularly about the 'tenuous' light cast by the candle flames? Why is their gloom called 'voluptuous'?

4 Look also at the ways in which the writer appeals to our senses in his writing. Choose examples and discuss them in the same way as you did with the comparisons in 2. Take each sense in turn and notice the way Laurie Lee makes it come alive in our imaginations as we read.

5 What do you learn of the narrator's mother from this passage? Perhaps the family described here remind you of yours in the evening, even though they may behave in a very different manner. Tell the rest of the class about them, trying to bring them to the class's imagination as clearly as Laurie Lee has brought his family to yours.

Composition

1 Write about your family in the evenings in the same way as Laurie Lee has done above. Look back at the work you have done before this and remember the exercises in using your senses and vivid comparisons in your writing, and read again Laurie Lee's description before starting yours.

2 At dusk or after dark go to a part of your house where you can be alone, or outside in the garden or street, and listen very carefully to all the noises around you, those close and those far away. Build your observations into a poem called 'Night Noises'.

3 Write a poem or prose description of the thoughts and feelings that come to you at night when you lie awake and hear the rest of the family sleeping, wonder what has caused that stair to creak, feel sure that your dressing gown hanging on the door is alive. . . .

4 Write a story that will continue from the scene described below:

Colin never knew what woke him. He lay on his back and stared at the moonlight. He had woken suddenly and completely, with no buffer of drowsiness to take the shock. His senses were needle-pointed, he was aware of every detail of the room, the pools of light and darkness shouted at him.

He got out of bed, and went to the window. It was a clear night, the air cold and sweet after the storm: the moon cast hard shadows over the farmyard. Scamp lay by the barn door, his head between his paws. Then Colin saw something move. He saw it only out of the corner of his eye, and it was gone in a moment, but he was never in any doubt: a shadow had slipped across the patch of moonlight that lay between the end of the house and the gate that led to the Riddings, the steep hill-field behind the farm.

'Hey! Scamp!' whispered Colin. The dog did not move. 'Hey! Wake up!' Scamp whined softly, and gave a muted yelp. 'Come on! Fetch him!' Scamp whined again, then crawled, barely raising his belly from the floor, into the barn. 'What on earth? Hey!' But Scamp would not come.

Colin pulled on his shirt and trousers over his pyjamas, and jammed his feet into a pair of shoes, before going to wake Gowther. But when he came to Susan's door he paused, and, for no reason that he could explain, opened the door. The bed was empty, the window open.

Colin tiptoed downstairs and groped his way to the door. It was still bolted. Had Susan dropped nine feet to the cobbles? He eased the bolts, and stepped outside, and as he looked he saw a thin silhouette pass over the skyline of the Riddings.

He struggled up the hill as fast as he could, but it was some time before he spotted the figure again, now moving across Clinton hill, a quarter of a mile away.

Colin ran: and by the time he stood at the top of Clinton hill he had halved the lead that Susan had gained. For it was undoubtedly Susan. She was wearing her pyjamas, and she seemed to glide smoothly over the ground, giving a strange impression that she was running, though her movements were those of walking. Straight ahead of her were the dark tops of the trees in the quarry.

'Sue!' No, wait. That's dangerous. She's sleep-walking. But she's heading for the quarry.

Colin ran as hard as he had ever run. Once he was off the hill-top the uneven ground hid Susan, but he knew the general direction. He came to the fence that stood on the edge of the highest cliff and looked around while he recovered his breath.

The moon showed all the hill-side and much of the quarry: the pump-tower gleamed, and the vanes turned. But Susan was nowhere to be seen. Colin leant against a fence-stump. She ought to be in sight: he could not have overtaken her: she must have reached here. Colin searched the sides of the quarry with his eyes, and looked at the smooth black mirror of the water. He was frightened. Where was she?

Then he cried out his fear as something slithered over his shoe and plucked at his ankle. He started back, and looked down. It was a hand. A ledge of earth, inches wide, ran along the other side of the fence and crumbled away to the rock face a few feet below: then the drop was sheer to the tarn-like water. The hand now clutched the ledge.

'Sue!'

He stretched over the barbed wire. She was right below him,

48

spread-eagled between the ledge and the cliff proper, her pale face turned up to his.

'Hang on! Oh, hang on!'

Colin threw himself flat on the ground, wrapped one arm round the stump, thrust the other under the wire, and grabbed at the hand. But though it looked like a hand, it felt like a hoof.

The wire tore Colin's sleeve as he shouted and snatched his arm away. Then, as Susan's face rose above the ledge, a foot from his own, and he saw the light that glowed in her eyes, Colin abandoned reason, thought. He shot backwards from the ledge, crouched, stumbled, fled. He looked back only once, and it seemed that out of the quarry a formless shadow was rising into the sky. Behind him the stars went out, but in their place were two red stars, unwinking, and close together.

Alan Garner, *The Moon of Gomrath*

5   Light thickens, and the crow
Makes wing to the rooky wood;
Good things of day begin to droop and drowse,
Whiles night's black agents to their preys do rouse.

William Shakespeare, *Macbeth*

Write a poem that dwells on the mystery and menace that surround you as dusk darkens into night. Stand outside one night, drinking in the atmosphere that closes around you—or let your imagination make it grow from a close study of the photograph.

Hide and Seek

Call out. Call loud: 'I'm ready! Come and find me!'
The sacks in the toolshed smell like the seaside.
They'll never find you in this salty dark,
But be careful that your feet aren't sticking out.
Wiser not to risk another shout.
The floor is cold. They'll probably be searching
The bushes near the swing. Whatever happens
You mustn't sneeze when they come prowling in.
And here they are, whispering at the door;
You've never heard them sound so hushed before.
Don't breathe. Don't move. Stay dumb. Hide in your blindness.
They're moving closer, someone stumbles, mutters;
Their words and laughter scuffle, and they're gone.
But don't come out just yet; they'll try the lane
And then the greenhouse and back here again.
They must be thinking that you're very clever,
Getting more puzzled as they search all over.
It seems a long time since they went away.
Your legs are stiff, the cold bites through your coat;
The dark damp smell of sand moves in your throat.
It's time to let them know that you're the winner.
Push off the sacks. Uncurl and stretch. That's better!
Out of the shed and call them: 'I've won!
Here I am! Come and own up I've caught you!'
The darkening garden watches. Nothing stirs.
The bushes hold their breath; the sun is gone.
Yes, here you are. But where are they who sought you?

Vernon Scannell

C Morning

Cock-crow

Out of the wood of thoughts that grows by night
To be cut down by the sharp axe of light,—
Out of the night, two cocks together crow,
Cleaving the darkness with a silver blow:
And bright before my eyes twin trumpeters stand,
Heralds of splendour, one at either hand,
Each facing each as in a coat of arms:
The milkers lace their boots up at the farms.

Edward Thomas

Composition

1 Describe the scene of a typical morning (in the same way as you described a typical evening in Section B) at home: start from the moment you wake up and describe your family at breakfast, the arrival of the newspaper/post/milkman, the rush to get off to work and school.
2 Now describe a memorable morning when everything went wrong and life seemed a waking nightmare.
3 Try to imagine the early morning through the eyes of another person, perhaps someone you know well, or someone you see regularly, like the milkman, postman, or, as in this passage, a paper boy:

The traffic was now continuous along the City Road, and there were queues at all the bus stops for buses into town. Billy passed them as he headed away from the city. He started to deliver at a row of detached houses and bungalows: pebble-dash and stone, and leaded windows. The row ended and he turned off the main road, up Firs Hill. The hill was steep. Trees had been planted at regular intervals along a cropped verge and the houses stood well back, shielded from the road, and from each other by trees and high wicker fences. Billy stopped before a wrought-iron gate with spikes at the top. On one of the gate-posts was a notice: No Hawkers No Callers. Billy looked down the drive and popped two squares of chocolate into his mouth. He left one half of the gate wide open and set off towards the house. Rhododendron shrubs crowded both sides of the drive, right up to the front door. He pushed the flap. It was stiff and the spring creaked. He looked towards the corners of the house, then eased the paper through and slowly lowered the flap until it clamped the paper. The curtains in all the front windows were drawn. The garden was wild, and moss and grass were replacing the asphalt on the drive. Billy used the moss and the grass like stepping stones until the last few yards, then he sprinted out, slamming the gate shut behind him. He unwrapped the last two squares of chocolate and looked back. A thrush ran out from under a rhododendron shrub and started to tug a worm from the soil between the loose asphalt chips. It stood over the worm and tugged vertically, exposing its speckled throat and pointing its beak to the sky. The worm stretched, but held. The thrush lowered its head and backed off, pulling at a more acute angle. The worm still held, so the thrush stepped in and jerked at the slack. The worm ripped out of the ground and the thrush ran away with it, back under the shrubs. Billy flicked the chocolate wrapper through the gate and passed on.

A milk dray whined up the hill, close to the kerb. Every time the near wheels dipped into a grate, the bottles rattled in their crates. It stopped and the driver jumped out of the cab whistling. He slid a crate off the back and carried it across the road. Billy glanced round as he approached the dray. There was no one else on the hill. He lifted a bottle of orange juice and a carton of eggs and popped them into his bag. When the driver returned, Billy was delivering papers at the next house. The dray passed him again further up. It stopped and the driver lit a cigarette, waiting for Billy to draw level.

'How's it going then, young un?'

Billy stopped and lolled back against the dray.

'O, not so bad.'

'Tha could do wi' some transport.'

He grinned and patted the dray.

'This is better than walking, tha knows.'

'Ar, only just, though.'

Billy kicked the back tyre.

'They only go about five miles an hour, these things.'

'It's still better than walking, isn't it?'

'I could go faster on a kid's scooter.'

The milkman nipped his cigarette out and blew on the end.

'You know what I always say?'

'What?'

'Third class riding's better than first class walking anyday.'

He tucked the tab into the breast pocket of his overalls and crossed the road, carrying two bottles in each hand. Billy watched him across the open back of the dray, then dipped into his bag for the orange. He held the bottle horizontally between thumb and little finger, then tilted it to make the air bubble travel the length of the bottle, and back again. Top to bottom, top to bottom, until the flakes raged like a glass snow storm. He punched his thumb through the cap, and downed the contents in two gulps, dropped the bottle back into a crate, and passed on up the hill.

A lane cut across the top of Firs Hill, forming a T-junction. Billy turned left along it. There was no pavement, and whenever a car approached he either crossed the lane or stepped into the long grass at the side and waited for it to pass. Fields, and a few hedgerow trees sloped down into the valley. Toy traffic travelled along the City Road, and across the road, in the valley bottom, was the sprawl of the estate. Towards the city, a pit chimney and the pit-head winding gear showed above the rooftops, and at the back of the estate was a patchwork of fields, black, and grey, and pale winter green; giving way to a wood, which stood out on the far slope as clear as an ink blot.

Billy pulled his jacket together as the wind murmured over the top of the moor, and across into the lane. But the zip was broken and the jacket fell open again. He crossed the lane and crouched down with his back against the wall. The stones were wet, and shone different shades of brown and green, like polished leather. Billy opened his bag and flicked through the contents. He pulled out the 'Dandy' and turned immediately to 'Desperate Dan'.

Dan is going to a wedding. His nephew and niece are helping him to get ready. His niece puts his top hat on the chair. *Crunch!* goes that hat as Dan sits on it. He goes to buy a new hat, but they are all FAR TOO SMALL. This is the biggest in the shop, the assistant tells him. Dan tries it on. It's almost big enough, he says, but when he tries to pull it down a bit, he rips the brim off and it comes down over his face. *OH, NO!* he says, looking over the brim. Outside the shop he has an idea, and points to something not shown in the picture. *Ah! That's the very thing!* he says, but first he has to clear the City Square so that no one will see what he is going to do. Round the corner, he bends over a water hydrant and blows. Water explodes out of the fountain in the square, drenching everybody, and they all have to go home, leaving the square deserted. Good, now I can get what I want, Dan says. In the next picture, Dan is trying on a big grey topper. He looks pleased and says, *That's it! And it fits a treat.* He attends the wedding, and at the Reception Hall he hands his hat to the cloakroom attendant. The attendant can't hold it and the hat goes *Crunch!* on his foot. *Ooyah!* goes the attendant. He tries to pick it up, saying, *Help! What a hat! It's made of solid stone!* The last picture shows

where the hat came from: WILLIAM SMITH, MAYOR OF CAC-
TUSVILLE 1865–86. SHOT AT HIGH NOON BY BLACK JAKE.

Billy stood up into the wind and flexed his knees as he
stepped back on to the lane. He started to run, holding the bag
under one arm to stop it slapping and dragging at his hip. He
delivered the 'Dandy' with a newspaper and several magazines
at a farmhouse. A collie barked at his heels all the way through
the yard, and back out again. It followed him along the lane,
then stopped and barked him out of sight over a rise. Billy
started to run again. He rolled a newspaper into a telescope
and spied through it as he ran. Until he spied a stone house,
standing back from the lane. Then he slowed to a walk, smooth-
ing out the newspaper and rolling it the other way to neutralize
the first curve.

At the side of the house, a grey Bentley was parked before
an open garage. Billy never took his eyes off it as he walked up
the drive, and when he reached the top, he veered across and
looked in at the dashboard. The front door of the house
opened, making him step back quickly from the car and turn
round. A man in a dark suit came out, followed by two little
girls in school uniform. They all climbed into the front of the
car, and the little girls waved to a woman in a dressing gown
standing at the door. Billy handed her the newspaper and looked
past her into the house. The hall and stairs were carpeted. A
radiator with a glass shelf ran along one wall, and on the shelf
stood a vase of fresh daffodils. The car freewheeled down the
drive and turned into the lane. The woman waved with the
newspaper and closed the door. . . . On the drive the tyres of
the car had imprinted two patterned bands, reminiscent of
markings on a snake's back.

Barry Hines, *A Kestrel for a Knave*

Before planning what you are going to write, discuss the
character of Billy as it emerges here. Does he enjoy his job?
What interests him on his round? What does the conversation
with the milkman tell us of him? What is conveyed by the way
he uses a newspaper as a telescope and uses 'the moss and
grass as stepping-stones'? Discuss in the same way all the other

details in the passage that tell us more of what he is like as a person. Why did the writer include the description of the 'Desperate Dan' story?

Start your composition by giving the person in your story a clearly-imagined character like Billy: don't state to the reader what these characteristics are, but let them emerge gradually in action through what your character does and says, in the same way as Barry Hines has done with Billy above.

Try to photograph your character's progress in the same way as the writer has done above — for instance, look back at what Barry Hines has written instead of

Billy noticed a thrush pulling at a worm   or

Billy drank the orange juice   or

He could see the town where he lived down in the valley below.

Concentrate on the scene, noticing such small but important details as the way the flap of a letter-box 'clamped' the paper, the colours brought out by rain in the stone of the houses, the way Billy's bag was 'slapping and dragging at his hip', the marks of the tyre like those 'on a snake's back'.

4 Describe your journey to school in similar detail, perhaps making it interesting by building it round an incident as Barry Hines has done — a meeting with someone on the way, for instance, or an event on the bus — describing a particular journey on a particular day. Describe people you see on the way, perhaps only glimpsed like someone waiting to cross the road or getting out of a car, perhaps seen regularly like a traffic warden.

5 Think back to your first journey to your present school and your impressions of it when you entered it for the first time. Describe your journey and arrival on *that* very special morning.

Action

1 Walk around the room as you did in Chapter 1 without touching one another.

2 Now you are walking to school. Meet your friends, park your bicycles at school, talk about the day's lessons and last night's homework, etc.

3 The School Bus. In groups of five to eight arrange a scene that will show the bus. Each of you play a clearly defined character, not yourself, and behave as this person would in real life.

4 Make **3** into a more interesting scene by building it around a crisis, e.g.

   the bus has a puncture or gets stuck in a snowdrift

   someone is taken ill

   an argument develops between the conductor and one of the passengers

Decide on what the situation is going to be and then repeat what you did in **3**, letting the crisis develop naturally and behaving as your character would throughout.

5 Read and discuss the writing you have done in response to the suggestions in the Composition section above, and

prepare a programme of your writing for performance to the rest of the class. Remember the work you did in Section A of Chapter 1 and how you made your programme interesting by varying the speakers, sometimes speaking independently and sometimes in pairs or as a group. Select the most interesting pieces (perhaps making extracts from some), and try out before your performance a recording of your programme for you to listen to and criticise in advance: you will then be able to judge for yourselves what has worked and what needs further rehearsal.

There may be time to add a similar programme made up from your Night pieces, to form a contrast, perhaps using the Edward Thomas poem at the beginning of this Section as a link between the two halves of your programme: you may find it similarly useful to include readings of excerpts from other passages printed in this chapter as links between your own writing.

Listen to the tapes made by the groups of the Morning (and perhaps Night) pieces. As a class select the best parts of each Morning programme and arrange them into a new order that will include parts of the scenes you improvised above, and adding further action that will help express what the writing says. Rehearse the combined programme of readings and action and perform it to another class.

3 Fire

A Fireweed

Action

1 Sit on the floor in groups and think of the noises made by fire: express them in single words. Build them up into a sound poem with the words placed in an order that will enact the growing of a fire and its gradually dying out. Some words will be repeated, and some parts will be said more quickly and more loudly than others. Don't plan it out through discussion first but let it build up spontaneously: then discuss how it can be improved, rehearse and finally tape it.

2 Now work out a pattern of words that describe the colours and shapes of the flames and smoke of the fire whose sounds you have just described. Rehearse it as you did in **1**.

3 Add movements to fit the movements of these shapes as you describe them.

4 Take away the words you used in **2** and enact the same sequence of movements to fit the tape you made in **1**, but keep the words you made in **2** in mind to help you.

5 **a** Perform your finished product to another group, and pool ideas as in earlier exercises.

b Work out a sound poem from the best ideas of both groups, and add percussion noises (besides using musical instruments, make up your own effective noises like rubbing two sheets of sandpaper together, clapping hands, etc.).

c One group form a ring round the other. Those in the

centre are the fire, while the group outside make a sound poem of words and noises.

d Change over and repeat.

e Now each double group can perform their piece to the rest of the class and the ideas of all the groups can be brought together for a large-scale fire involving all the class.

Composition

1 Watch fire closely and describe it as accurately as you can. Watch it in different forms: a lighted match, a candle flame, a bonfire, a wood or coal fire, a piece of burning paper, a cigarette, a firework. Note down the exact words or comparisons to describe its shape, colour, noise and smell; then build your notes into a careful description, perhaps in a poem whose rhythm imitates the movement of the fire, as Louis Untermeyer has done in his description of a coal fire:

See how its little hands reach here and there,
Finger the air;
Then, growing bolder, twisting free,
It fastens on the remnant of the tree
and, one by one,
Consumes them, mounts beyond them, leaps, is done,
And goes back to the sun.

2 Write about Guy Fawkes' Night, making use of the descriptions you made in 1 to give your account greater vividness and accuracy. Focus on the bonfire and the fireworks.

3 Find out more about Guy Fawkes and what happened on the first November 5th. Write a story or play based on your research. Try to see this familiar story from a new viewpoint—for instance, make the central character of your play someone who lives near the house where the conspirators meet, and overhears their plans. Should he tell the authorities?...

4 Write about the morning after Guy Fawkes' Night, about your feelings as you look at the scene of the previous night's excitement and fun, as I did in this poem:

Winter breathes on the ashes of autumn,
Stirring up half-forgotten images:
The hissing flames that leap and snarl,
The soft radiance that holds an alien
Group apart in their solitary ritual,

While we stand, watching them,
Poised on the brink of night,
Fighting the cold with jokes and
Hot potato that tastes of gunpowder.
This moment is ours to hold, warming
Cold fingers — but soon the flame
Wavers, the neighbours are invisible,
And the shuddering weeds watch
While winter pokes the fire out
And murmurs an old song.

5 Imagine primitive man discovering fire. Describe what you
think happened and imagine the reactions of his neighbours
to this new invention. Show how you think he discovered it
could be used to give comfort to their lives, but how he
still respected its power.

6 Here is another extract from 'The Moon of Gomrath'.

Colin followed Susan up the bare slope of the Beacon, and
they sat on the stone blocks at the top. He pointed out the
line of the track as accurately as he could remember it. Then
it was a matter of waiting for the moon, and before long the
children were both bored and cold.

'Have you got a match with you?' said Susan.

'No, I don't think so.'

'Well, have a look.'

Colin turned out his pockets, and at the bottom of the fluff,
crumbs, and balls of silver paper he found one grubby match-
stick.

'Do you think it's safe to light a fire?' said Colin.

'It should be. There aren't any trees here, and this sand will
stop it from spreading.'

The children gathered kindling of rowan twigs, and among
the trees at the bottom of the hill they found a naked, long-
fallen pine, as smooth as bone.

'Don't build it too dense,' said Susan, 'or it won't start.'

From match to twig to branch the light grew, until the pine
wood spurted fire. The flames leapt high, and within seconds

the whole pile roared. Colin and Susan threw the wood they had gathered on to the flames, but the more they threw, the faster the wood burnt.

'Steady,' said Colin. 'It'll get out of control if we don't watch it. There's too much resin in the wood.'

But Susan was carried away by the urgency of the fire. She ran down to the pine tree, and began to pull on a heavier branch.

'Here, come and give me a hand, Colin! This'll make it really go!'

'No!' Colin's voice was suddenly tense. 'Don't put any more on. There's something wrong. I'm cold.'

'It's only the wind,' said Susan. 'Oh, do hurry! There'll be nothing left!'

She swung all her weight on the branch, and stumbled as it broke from the trunk. Then she started to drag the branch backwards up the hill. Colin ran to her, and caught hold of her arm.

'Sue! Can't you feel it? It's not giving out any heat!'

'Who now brings fire to the mound at the Eve of Gomrath?' said a cold, thin voice behind them.

Colin and Susan turned.

The flames were a scarlet curtain between hill and sky, and within them, and a part of them, were three men. At first their tall shapes and haggard faces danced and merged with the blazing pine branches, and were as unstable as any picture that the mind sees in the shadows of a fire: but even while the children looked, they became more solid, rounded, and independent of the flames through which they stared. Then they were real, and terrible.

They were dressed all in red: red were their tunics, and red their cloaks; red their eyes, and red their long manes of hair bound back with circlets of red gold; three red shields on their backs, and three red spears in their hands; three red horses under them, and red was the harness. Red were they all, weapons and clothing and hair, both horses and men.

'Who — who are you?' whispered Colin. 'What do you want?'

The middle horseman stood in his saddle, and raised a glowing spear above his head.

'Lo, my son, great the news! Wakeful are the steeds we ride, the steeds from the ancient mound. Wakeful are we, the Horsemen of Donn, Einheriar of the Herlathing. Lo, my son!'

And he threw his spear high in the air. It flashed four times, and he caught it and brandished it in front of him. Then the three horsemen rode slowly out of the fire, and the flames splashed from them to the ground like red mercury. They loomed black against the glare of the hilltop, but ragged beards of light still played along the heads of their spears.

'Run,' said Colin to Susan.

But they were not half-way to the trees before there was a drumming of hoofs, a flutter of cloaks, and Colin and Susan were hooked off their feet by steel-sinewed arms and thrown across the necks of horses that hurled themselves through the night as though world's ruin were at their heels.

Alan Garner

Develop the fantasy as your imagination wills.

7 Write a story or play based on the sequence of photographs that follows.

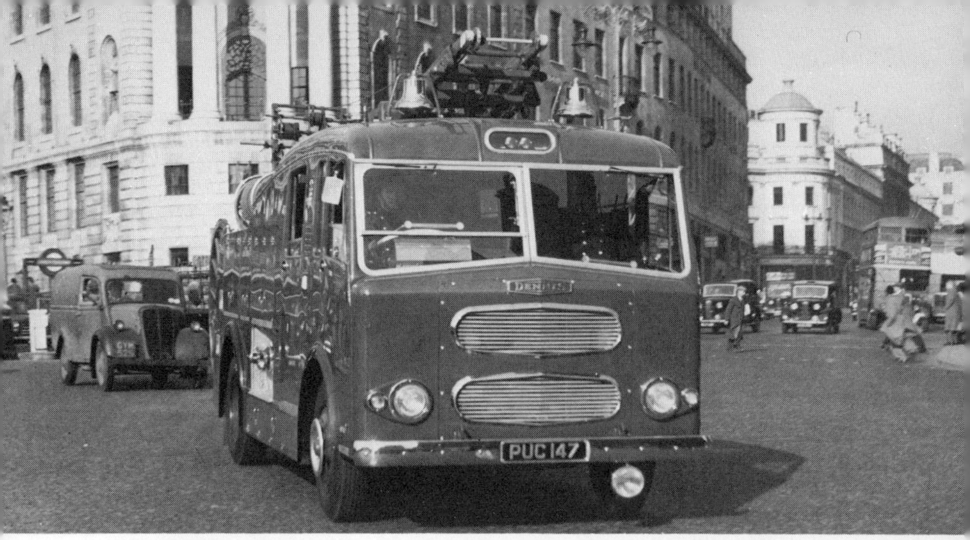
PUC 147

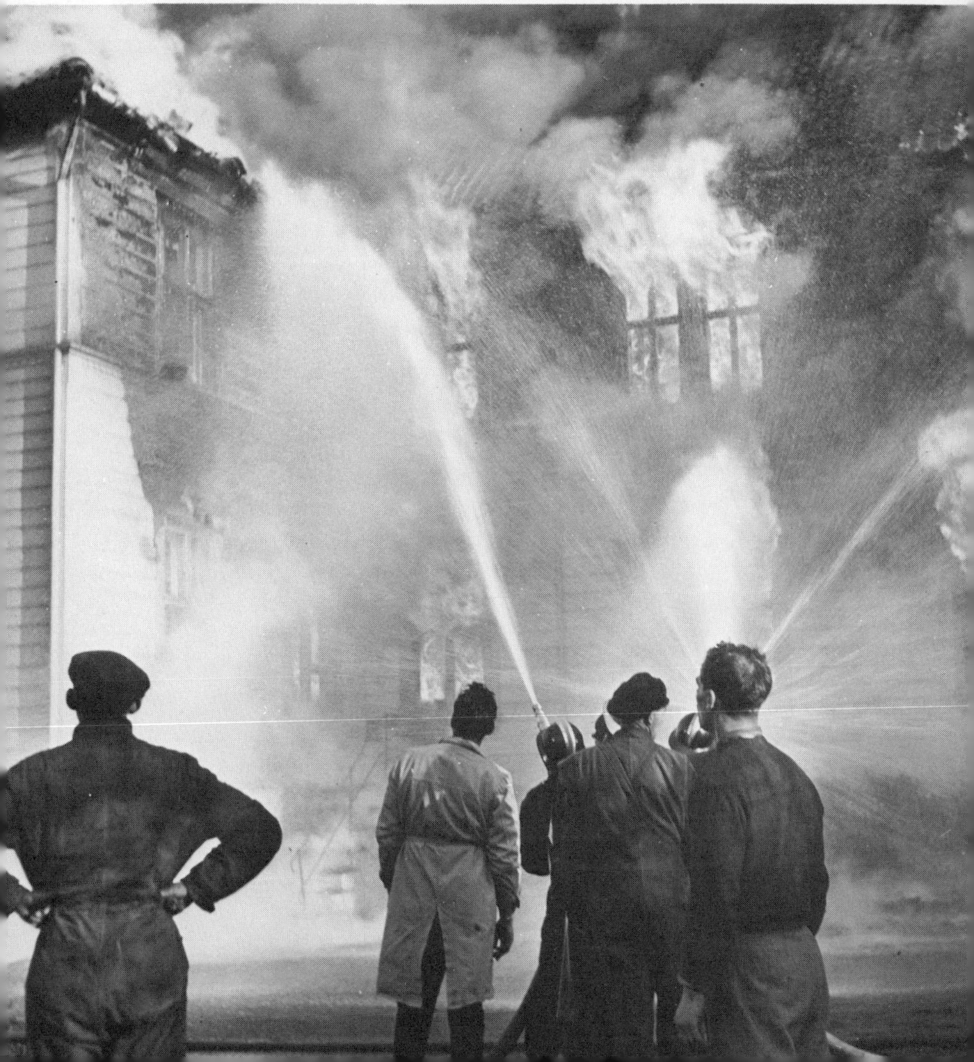

8 Develop the following situation, having first discussed the characters of the boys as they emerge here and making sure that what they say and do is consistent with what is revealed of them here. The scene is the outback in Australia.

The boys walked on along the road to Tinley in the blistering heat of the sun, and their packs became heavier and their pace slower. Sometimes they sat in the shade to cool off and to ease their shoulders. More cars stopped to offer them a lift, but each of them they waved on. They were on their own. They wanted no one.

For their lunch they dug a shallow hole and gathered sticks and made a small fire at the roadside to grill their sausages and boil water for instant coffee. Coffee, they felt, good and strong, was the sort of drink a fellow would have when he lived on his own, when he was a man. The water hadn't even started bubbling in the billy-can, the sausages were not even spitting, when a car pulled up and a woman called to them: 'Put that fire out!'

The boys stared at her. She looked like an angry school-mistress. 'You heard me,' she said. 'Put it out.'

'We're only havin' our lunch, lady,' said Wallace. 'What's wrong with that?'

'You boys are old enough to know better. Put it out at once or I'll report you to the police. There's a £200 fine and a jail sentence for lighting a fire in the open on a day like this.'

'Crikey, it's only a little fire,' complained Wallace. 'We've dug a hole an' all. We're watching it.'

'Put it out quickly. Tip your water over it.'

'Fair go, lady,' said Wallace. 'What are we supposed to drink? It's a hot day.'

It was Harry who lifted the billy off with a stick and emptied the water into the hole, for he had suddenly become aware of the heat and the strength of the north wind, of the way it fanned the flames, of the way the smoke scattered.

'Now stamp on it,' the woman called. 'Get it out. The last spark. Put it all out.'

She watched them with a set face until they had done it; then she said, 'If you want hot water on a day like this, go into a house somewhere and ask for it nicely. Fire is a dangerous plaything at this time of the year. Don't forget it.'

She drove on, and the boys were left looking at one another glumly. 'Plaything, my fat aunt,' said Wallace.

'Wouldn't it make you sick?' snorted Graham.

'I suppose she was right, though,' said Harry.

'We were watchin' it. It couldn't have done any harm.' Wallace was very upset. 'If we can't light a fire, what are we goin' to eat and drink? What about our sausages an' all?'

'I don't know,' said Graham.

'It's *stupid*. All right for her. She can go home and switch on the stove. Grown-ups. You can't get away from them. Two hundred pound fine for cookin' your lunch! Go to jail for drinkin' coffee! I suppose we're expected to starve to death.'

'We've got some buns,' said Harry.

'*Buns!*'

'And we can drink water.'

'Whose side are you on? I want *coffee* and *sausages*.'

Another car heading in the opposite direction pulled up. It was a utility truck, and at the wheel was a man who looked like a farmer. 'You boys aren't lighting a fire, are you?' he said.

'No,' said Wallace sullenly.

'Make sure you don't.'

They had buns for lunch, and water. Much of the magic of the day had already gone sour on them. . . .

Soon enough the resentment eased out of the boys. They were too young and too free at heart to be miserable for long. Each had several pounds in his pocket (saved over a period of months), and they felt like millionaires. When they got to Tinley they bought pies and cokes and ice creams to fill up on and more buns and more sausages to take away with them, and for a few shillings a tiny heater, no larger than a shoe-polish tin, that burned methylated spirits with a hot blue flame and no smoke. 'Works just like a gas stove,' the man in the shop said. 'Clear the ground, scoop out a hole, put some stones around it to break the wind and it'll be as safe as houses.'

They hadn't gone much more than a mile beyond Tinley towards the ranges when Wallace said, 'I'm dog-tired. Let's find a creek or somethin' and camp.'

'Good idea,' said Graham, thankfully, for he never would have suggested it himself.

They fried sausages and made coffee, and talked, and swatted at mosquitoes, and watched the stars come out, and listened to the hot dry wind creaking and crackling through the trees. Then they shone their torches into the undergrowth and up over their heads through the foliage. Insects glowed and flickered in the beams. 'Light bends, you know,' said Harry, waving his torch from side to side. 'But it won't bend for me.'

They hadn't bothered to put the tent up; they wriggled into their sleeping-bags in the open.

'Hope it doesn't rain,' said Graham.

Listening to voices, even one's own, was sort of nice in the dark.

'My dad says it won't rain for a month.' (That came from Harry.)

'Hot, isn't it?' (Graham again, though that one or another

should say it was not important. That the words should keep going was the thing.)

'Stinkin' hot,' agreed Wallace.

'These sleeping-bags'll be like ovens before long.'

'Better than bein' eaten by the mozzies.'

'I've got some repellent if you want it.'

'Beaut, isn't it, bein' on our own?'

'Super.'

'Makes you feel good. I don't mean goodie-goodie. You know, *good*.'

'Tough?'

'Yeh. In a way.'

'Better chuck us that repellent.'

'Makes you feel as though you'd like to do something you've never done before.'

'Like what?'

'I don't know. Like somethin' different. Like somethin' that'd get your name in the papers. . . .'

Wallace was half-awake, half-asleep. He had been asleep for a while, but had become partly aware of his surroundings again, of the wind and the heat. He was wet with perspiration. Graham had been right about sleeping-bags and ovens. Wallace felt that he was being cooked, and his right hip was bruised and sore. He had dug a little hole for his hip, but he must have turned away from it. The trouble was, he couldn't completely wake up. He was in a sort of limbo of acute discomfort but was too hazy in the head to do anything about it.

When at last he managed to open his eyes he became aware of a faint glow. He thought he could smell methylated spirits. He even thought he could see Graham.

'Is that you?' he said.

'Yes,' said Graham.

'What are you doin'?'

'Making coffee.'

Wallace sat up, panting. He felt giddy. 'What are you makin' coffee for?'

'I'm thirsty. Do you want a cup?'

'What's the time?'

'Twenty past one.'

'Yeh. I'll have a cup.'

Wallace peeled his sleeping-bag down to the waist, and felt better. 'Twenty past one!'

'About that.'

'Harry's sleepin' all right.'

'Trust Harry,' said Graham. 'He could sleep anywhere.'

Wallace thought he had heard something like that before, but couldn't remember when. 'Funny in the bush at night, isn't it? Awful dark.'

'Noisy too. I heard a tree fall down. Not far away either. Woke me up.'

'It's the wind.'

'Guess so.'

'Stinkin' hot, isn't it?'

'You can say that again. But this water's awful slow coming to the boil.'

'The wind, I suppose.'

'It's taken two lots of metho already,' said Graham.

'Have you got the lid on?'

'Can't see when it boils if you've got the lid on.'

'Put the lid on, I reckon, or it'll never boil.'

'Don't know where the lid is, do you?'

'*Feel* for it. It's there somewhere. Use your torch.'

'The battery's flat. Bloomin' thing. Must have been a crook battery. Hardly used it at all. *Now* look what I've done! That's the metho bottle knocked for six.'

'You dope,' cried Wallace. 'Pick it up quick. Or we'll lose it all.'

'The cork's in it.' Graham groped for it, feeling a bit of a fool, and said, 'Crumbs.'

'Now what?'

'The cork's *not* in it, that's what. It must have come out.'

'How could it come out? Honest to goodness—'

'It's *burning*,' howled Graham.

A blue flame snaked from the little heater up through the rocks towards the bottle in the boy's hand; or at least that was how it seemed to happen. It happened so swiftly it may have deceived the eye. Instinctively, to protect himself, Graham threw the bottle away. There was a shower of fire from its neck, as from the nozzle of a hose.

'Oh my gosh,' yelled Wallace, and tore off his sleeping-bag. 'Harry!' he screamed. 'Wake up, Harry!'

They tried to stamp on the fire, but their feet were bare and they couldn't find their shoes. They tried to smother it with their sleeping-bags, but *it* seemed to be everywhere. Harry couldn't even escape from his bag; he couldn't find the zip fastener, and for a few awful moments in his confusion between sleep and wakefulness he thought he was in his bed at home and the house had burst into flames around him. He couldn't come to grips with the situation; he knew only dismay and the wildest kind of alarm. Graham and Wallace, panicking, were throwing themselves from place to place, almost sobbing, beating futilely at a widening arc of fire. Every desperate blow they made seemed to fan the fire, to scatter it farther, to feed it.

'Put it out,' shouted Graham. 'Put it out.'

It wasn't dark any longer. It was a flickering world of tree trunks and twisted boughs, of scrub and saplings and stones, of shouts and wind and smoke and frantic fear. It was so quick. It was terrible.

'Put it out,' cried Graham, and Harry fought out of his sleeping-bag, knowing somehow that they'd never get it out by beating at it, that they'd have to get water up from the creek. But all they had was a four-pint billy-can.

The fire was getting away from them in all directions, crackling through the scrub downwind, burning fiercely back into the wind. Even the ground was burning; grass, roots, and fallen

leaves were burning, humus was burning. There were flames on the trees, bark was burning, foliage was flaring, flaring like a whip-crack; and the heat was savage and searing and awful to breathe.

'We can't, we can't,' cried Wallace. 'What are we going to do?'

They beat at it and beat at it and beat at it.

'Oh gee,' sobbed Graham. He was crying, and he hadn't cried since he was twelve years old. 'What have I done? *We've got to get it out!*'

Harry was scrambling around wildly, bundling all their things together. It was not that he was more level-headed than the others; it was just that he could see the end more clearly, the hopelessness of it, the absolute certainty of it, the imminent danger of encirclement, the possibility that they might be burnt alive. He could see all this because he hadn't been in it at the start. He wasn't responsible; he hadn't done it; and now that he was wide awake he could see it more clearly. He screamed at them: 'Grab your stuff and run for it.' But they didn't hear him or didn't want to hear him. They were blackened, their feet were cut, even their hair was singed. They beat and beat, and fire was leaping into the tree-tops, and there were no black shadows left, only bright light, red light, yellow light, light that was hard and cruel and terrifying, and there was a rushing sound, a roaring sound, explosions, and smoke, smoke like a red hot fog.

'No,' cried Graham. 'No, no, no.' His arms dropped to his sides and he shook with sobs and Wallace dragged him away. 'Oh, Wally,' he sobbed. 'What have I done?'

'We've got to get out of here,' shouted Harry. 'Grab the things and run.'

'Our shoes?' cried Wallace. 'Where are they?'

'I don't know. I don't know.'

'We've got to find our shoes.'

'They'll kill us,' sobbed Graham. 'They'll kill us. It's a terrible thing, an awful thing to have done.'

'Where'd we put our shoes?' Wallace was running around in circles, blindly. He didn't really know what he was doing. Everything had happened so quickly, so suddenly.

'For Pete's sake run!' shouted Harry.

Something in his voice seemed to get through to Wallace and Graham, and they ran, the three of them, like frightened rabbits. They ran this way and that, hugging their packs and their scorched sleeping-bags, blundering into the scrub, even into the trunks of trees. Fire and confusion seemed to be all around them. The fire's rays darted through the bush; it was like an endless chain with a will of its own, encircling and entangling them, or like a wall that leapt out of the earth to block every fresh run they made for safety. Even the creek couldn't help them. They didn't know where it was. There might as well not have been a creek at all.

'This way,' shouted Harry. 'A track.'

They stumbled back down the track towards Tinley; at least they thought it was towards Tinley, they didn't really know. Perhaps they were running to save their lives, running simply from fear, running away from what they had done.

When they thought they were safe they hid in the bush close to a partly constructed house. They could hear sirens wailing; lights were coming on here and there; the headlamps of cars were beaming and sweeping around curves in the track. They could hear shouts on the wind, they heard a woman cry hysterically, they heard Graham sobbing.

Over all was a red glow.

Ivan Southall

9 Read one another's stories in groups. Discuss which are the most realistic—in the action and dialogue of the characters, the description of the fire, and in their ideas of what will follow on from the situation described above. In your groups, improvise or write a play based on the extract from the novel and the best ideas that have emerged in your discussion. Then rehearse and perform it to the rest of the class. Perhaps you will wish to compose other scenes to show the fire's effect on other people—the townsfolk of Tinley, the families of boys, the man who sold the boys the stove, the lady who had told them to put their first fire out, etc.

10 Write a story about a fire getting out of control based on a similar situation to the one described by Ivan Southall,

perhaps an item you have heard about recently in the news, or even an event from your own experience. If you prefer, use one of the following suggestions as starting-points for a completely imaginary event:

a A group of children camping (perhaps at a Scout or Guide Camp) in an area that is a similar fire risk in the summer, like the New Forest. A forest fire starts, perhaps because of their carelessness, but perhaps because of a nearby group of wandering tinkers, of whom the children have been suspicious (or even frightened) before. . . .

b A night-watchman in a large factory is dozing. A few minutes ago he thought he heard a noise, and now he thinks he can smell something burning. Perhaps he is dreaming . . . but perhaps not. . . .

c A group of villagers in Sicily are watching the mountain above them anxiously, for it is Mount Etna, and scientists have predicted that the volcano will erupt again any day now. It is 4 a.m. The first traces of dawn are breaking the darkness. You have been awake all night, too frightened to sleep. It is cold, and you are shivering. You talk about the mountain's past angry eruptions. Only a miracle can save your village if the volcano erupts again. And now the ground is shivering too. . . .

d The captain of an oil tanker is directing his huge ship into the English Channel. It is night, and he can only make out the dim outline of the coast, but the occasional twinkling light makes him think of home, which is not far away now after a voyage of thousands of miles. Once this shipment of oil is unloaded he can face a month of uninterrupted relaxation with his family and friends: he has been away from them for three months now. . . . His dreams are abruptly shattered by an ear-splitting explosion. . . .

e A spaceship is approaching Mars. Earth is years away. The astronauts are weary of their seemingly endless journey. The mission is no longer exciting, but seems pointless somehow, especially when they think of how they will be ten years older when they see home again. They quarrel over trivial matters, and seem to be losing their grip . . . so, when a retro-rocket engine bursts into flame, can they cope?

Research and Discussion

1 Find out about primitive societies that worshipped the sun. What have the Incas and Stonehenge in common?
2 Read one another's stories written in response to **5** in the Composition section above, and discuss the reactions to the discovery of fire that you have imagined there. Try to imagine what life would be like without fire and analyse its importance in our lives.

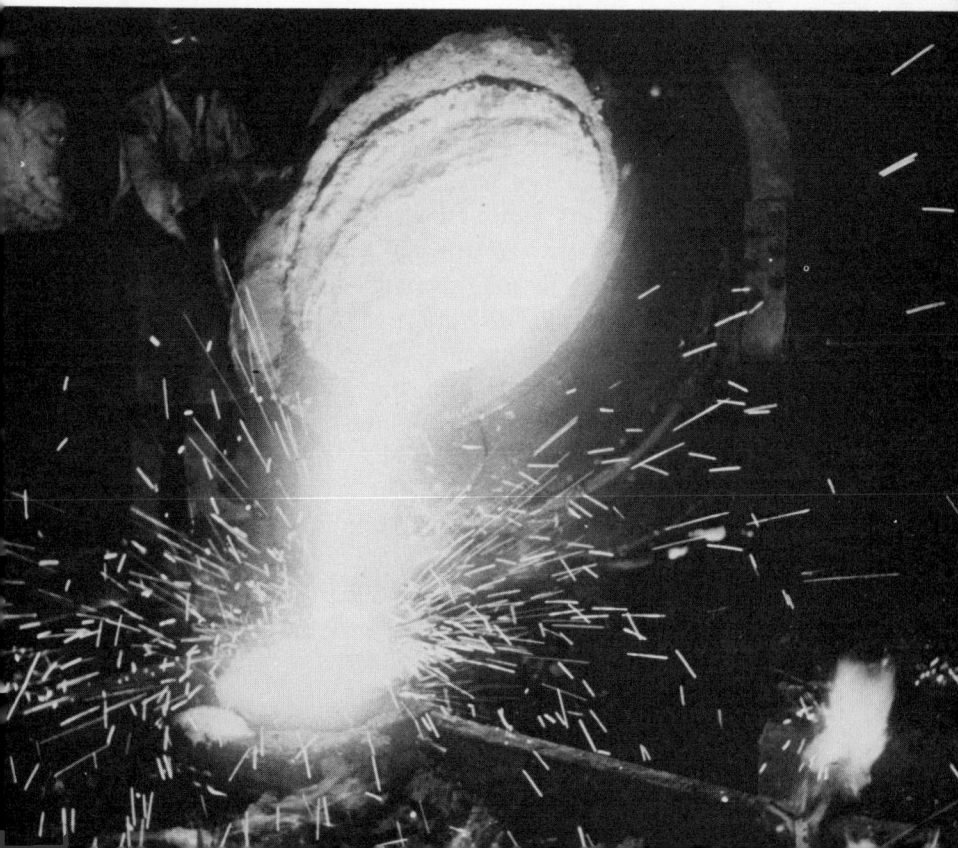

3 Find out as much as you can about the industrial uses of fire.
4 Find out about the devastation caused by fire: for instance, in the Great Fire of London, the timber fires in heavily-forested areas like Canada, the fires caused by bombing in the Second World War, the fires of intolerance that burned so-called witches like Joan of Arc. . . . Which other instances would you add to this list?
5 Is fire a blessing or a curse? Use what you have found out through research as the basis for your discussion.

Action

In groups of four, read again your stories about the discovery of fire. Then:
1 Pool your ideas and build up a play about the discovery of fire. Let the climax be your using it to make a sacrifice to the greater fire of the Sun.
2 Find out about the story of Prometheus and build up a play or dance drama about him.
3 Read the following, dividing the parts among you. I have based it on the story of Phaethon, whose father was Phoebus, the sun god, pictured by the Ancient Greeks as driving a fiery chariot pulled by a team of horses across the sky. Other mortals don't believe Phaethon when he tells them who his father is, so when Phoebus promises to grant his son any wish he may demand, Phaethon asks if he can drive the chariot one day to prove to his enemies whose son he really is. Phoebus tries to dissuade his son, for this task is too great for any mortal, but when he sees how upset Phaethon is, he allows his judgment to be overruled, with disastrous consequences. . . .

PHAETHON   The reins seem to leap in my throbbing hands.
            Thank you, father, for this favour you grant me.
            You need not fear: see! your proud steeds

Chafe and paw the dull earth,
Eyes fierce, nostrils quivering fire.
Let the Gates open and Day begin!

The morning crouches before us, waiting
For us to trace the broad arch of its spine.
Up, my beauties! The hot wind jingles
Their sparkling harness, fingers my hair.
How good it is to see the earth's slow
    curve
Fall away from me: the heavens are mine.

VOICE 1   But the proud boy's joy soon tenses into
                        alarm:

VOICE 2   His chariot is too light for the horses'
                        tug—

VOICE 3   It lurches and sways like a ship in a storm,

VOICE 1   Frightening the horses who buck and pull,

VOICES 2 and 3 Dragging his course up the tracks of the
                        stars.

ALL   The heavens are truly his now.

VOICE 1   But the earth smooths its contours into a
                        ball that
Hangs blue, far, far away,

VOICE 2   Growing slowly darker as he gathers
Speed.

PHAETHON   Father, where are you?

VOICE 3   His cries are drowned in the wind's
                        scream.

VOICE 1   The horses pant, eyes bulging terror.

VOICE 2   He stands trembling, reins limp
In his weakening grip as he stares at no-
                        thing,
Lost in the mists of fear.

PHAETHON   Help me!

VOICE 3   The zodiac reels into his path. He skids
Past huge beasts, hurtles through terror,
                        until,

VOICE 1   Catching his breath,

VOICE 2   he looks behind him
To see

VOICE 3	the Scorpion's black poison
ALL	Slowly swerve towards him on the out-stretched curve of its
	Tail, its cruel pincers poised to pluck out his eyes.
VOICE 1	With a scream he ducks,
VOICE 2	dropping the reins
VOICE 3	To throw his hands before his face.
PHAETHON	Father!
VOICE 1	The horses shy and seem to stand
	Still on the whistling air.
VOICE 2	Nothing
	Holds them now.
VOICE 3	Down
ALL	Down
	They plunge, tails stretched, teeth bared.

VOICE 1	Now Phaethon clings to the chariot's sides.
VOICE 2	The earth's curve spreads out flat again, Showing crags and oceans.
VOICE 3	The chariot Rips through smouldering clouds,
VOICE 1	sets fire To crops and mountains,
VOICE 2	whitens grass and Scars cracks in the earth's crust.
VOICE 3	The oceans boil.
PHAETHON	Dear father, help me! I'm a furnace. My feet are white hot, my cheeks Scorched with flying sparks. I can Scarcely breathe. My parched throat Chokes on thick black smoke. Where am I? Where are you, father? Where?
VOICE 1	Cities catch flame and steaming seas Become deserts littered with dead fish.
VOICE 2	The charred people cry out their pain,
VOICES 2 and 3	Their voices joining to form
ALL	one clamour— The great call to their father, Zeus:
VOICE 1	Father
VOICE 2	hear our prayer,
VOICE 3	spare us From this fire,
ALL	we beseech thee.
VOICE 1	The earth's prayer is answered.
VOICE 2	The orange sky Splits open.
VOICE 3	A fiercer fire plummets Down as
VOICE 1	Zeus's thunderbolt Knocks Phaethon clear.
VOICE 2	He falls in a long Scream,
VOICE 3	his red hair
ALL	hissing into the far horizons.

4 Now rehearse it for performance, adding sound effects (and perhaps music) as you did in your work at the beginning of this chapter, for a tape recording or live performance with movement.

5 Write between you four further sections to this poem (perhaps each member of the group contributing one of the sections), describing in fuller detail

   a how Phaethon goes to his father, Phoebus, demanding the use of his chariot, how his father tries to dissuade him, but eventually agrees;

   b his father's thoughts and fears as he watches what happens to his son;

   c more conversation between i mortals on earth wondering what is happening to them, and ii the gods—leading to Zeus's decision to hurl his thunderbolt;

   d Phaethon's thoughts as he hurtles towards the sea.

Add a and d to the beginning and end of the script above, and fit in various parts of b and c at appropriate moments in the script, giving a more varied effect.

You may prefer to have two groups combining, selecting the best writing for a final script, and thus have more voices for Phoebus, other gods, and other mortals, before rehearsing and then recording or performing it.

B Rutupiae light

Composition

Fire is also used as a signal. Rosemary Sutcliff's novel, *The Lantern Bearers*, opens with the departure of the last of the Roman Auxiliaries, leaving Britain to face the menace of invasion by the Saxon hordes. A young Roman officer decides at the last moment that his loyalties lie with Britain rather than the Legions:

And now the last feverish hours of getting the horses into the transports were over, and the men had been marched aboard while the brazen orders of the trumpets rang above the ordered tumult; and there was scarcely anything more to do. A flamed and feathered sunset was fading behind the Great Forest, and the tide was almost at the flood, running far up the creeks and inlets and winding waterways; and amid the last ordered coming and going, Aquila stood on the lifting deck of the *Clytemnestra*. The stern and mast-head lanterns were alight already, as the daylight dimmed, and any moment now the great fire-beacon on the crest of the Pharos should have sprung to life. But there would be no Rutupiae Light tonight to guide the fleets of the Empire. The last of the Eagles were flying from Britain. Any moment now the trumpets would sound as the Commandant came down from the Watergate and stepped on board, and the landing-bridge would be raised, and the Hortator's hammer would begin the steady, remorseless clack-clack-clack that beat out the time for the slaves on the rowing benches.

Aquila suddenly saw himself going to the Commandant in that last moment, laying his drawn sword at his feet, saying, 'Sir, everything is in order. Now let me go.' Would Callistus think that he was mad or hysterical? No, oddly enough—for there had never been a word between them save in the way of duty—he knew that Callistus would understand; but he knew also that Callistus would have no choice but to refuse. The choice was his. Quite clearly and coldly, in the still moment after the three days' turmoil, he knew that he must make it alone.

He turned to his old, grey-whiskered optio beside him, who had taught him all that he knew of soldiering, all that he knew of the handling of a troop—he had been so proud of his troop —and gripped his leather-clad shoulder an instant.

'God keep you Aemilius. I'll be back.'

He turned to the head of the landing-bridge and crossed over, quickly and openly as though in obedience to some last-moment order. No chance to bid good-bye to Felix, none to take leave of Nestor, his horse. He strode by the last remaining figures on the jetty, the native dockyard hands, no one particularly noticing him in the fading light, back through the Watergate into the desolate fort.

Everything in him felt bruised and bleeding. He had been bred a soldier, coming of a line of soldiers, and he was breaking faith with all the gods of his kind. Going 'wilful missing'. The very words had the sorry sound of disgrace. He was failing the men of his own troop, which seemed to him in that moment a worse thing than all else. Yet he did not turn back again to the waiting galleys. He knew that what he was doing was a thing that you couldn't judge for other people, only for yourself; and for himself, he did not know if it was the right thing, but he knew that it was the only thing.

He was scarcely aware of his direction, until he found himself at the foot of the Pharos. The ramp for the fuel-carts led steeply upward to the vast plinth, and at the head of it the mouth of the covered way gaped dark and empty in the gathering dusk. He mounted the ramp quickly and strode forward into the darkness. He was in the square hollowness of the tower foot where the fuel-carts were housed. The carts were there now, ranged side by side, mere blots of darkness in the lesser darkness. The dry, musty smell of baled straw was in his nostrils, and the sharp tang of pitch that had soaked into the stones of the walls. He turned to the narrow stairway that wound up the wall like the spiral twist of a snail shell, and began to climb.

He was only half-way up when he heard, faintly through the thick walls from the world outside, the trumpets sounding the Commandant on board. Any moment now he would be missed. Well, they would have little time for searching. They would not miss the tide for one junior officer gone wilful missing. He climbed on, up and up, stumbling a little, through chamber after chamber, with the sense of height increasing on him, past the deserted quarters where the men on beacon duty had lived like peregrine falcons high above the world. The grey dusk seeping through the small windows showed the dark shapes of the debris they had left behind them—rough wooden furniture and cast-off gear, like the stranded flotsam on the shore left when the tide flows out, as Rome's tide was flowing out. Up and up until the stairway ran out into open air, and he ducked at last through a little low-set doorway into complete darkness, into the 'Immediate Use' fuel store just below the signal platform. Feeling with outstretched hands, he found the ranged barrels of pitch, the straw and brushwood and stacked logs. A gap opened to his questing hand between the brushwood and the wall, and he crawled into it and crouched there, pulling the brushwood over again behind him.

It wasn't a good hiding-place, but the tide would be already on the turn.

For what seemed a very long time he crouched there, his heart beating in slow, uneven drubs. From far, far below him, in another world, he thought he heard the tramp of mailed sandals, and voices that shouted his name. He wondered what he should do if they came up here and found him, skulking like a cornered rat under a garbage pile; but the time passed, and the footsteps and the calling voices came and went, hurrying, but never mounted the stairs of the forsaken tower. And presently the trumpets sounded again, recalling the searchers lest they lose the tide. Too late now to change his mind.

More time passed, and he knew that the galleys would be slipping down the broad river-way between the marshes. And then once more he heard the trumpets. No, only one. The call was faint, faint as the echo of a seabird's cry; but Aquila's ear caught the sad, familiar notes of the call. In one of those galleys slipping seaward, somebody, in savage comment on what had happened, or merely in farewell, was sounding 'Lights Out'.

And now that it was all over, now that the choice was made, and one faith kept and one faith broken, Aquila drove his face down on to his forearm against the whippy roughness of the brushwood bundles, and cried as he had never cried before and would never cry again.

A long while later he turned himself about in his hiding-place, and ducked out on to the narrow stairway, spent and empty as though he had cried his heart away. Dusk had long since deepened into the dark, and the cold moonlight came down the steps from the beacon platform, plashing silvery from step to step. And as he checked there, leaning against the wall, the silence of the great fortress came up to him, a silence of desolation and complete emptiness. On a sudden impulse he turned upward towards the moonlight instead of down into the blackness that swallowed the descending stairway, and stumbled up the last few steps, emerging on the beacon platform.

The moon was riding high in a sky pearled and feathered with high wind-cloud, and a little wind sighed across the breast-high parapet with a faint aeolian hum through the iron-work of the beacon tripod. The brazier was made up ready for lighting, with fuel stacked beside it, as it had been stacked every night. Aquila crossed to the parapet and stood looking down. There were lights in the little ragged town that huddled against the fortress walls, but the great fort below him was empty and still in the moonlight as a ruin that had been hearth-cold for a hundred years. Presently, in the daylight, men would come and strip the place of whatever was useful for them, but probably after dark they would leave it empty and forsaken to its ghosts. Would they be the ghosts of the men who had sailed on this tide? Or of the men who had left their names on the leaning gravestones above the wash of the tide? A Cohort Centurion with a Syrian name, dying after thirty years' service, a boy trumpeter of the Second Legion, dying after two. . . .

Aquila's gaze lengthened out across the marshes in the wake of the galleys, and far out to sea he thought that he could still make out a spark of light. The stern lantern of a transport; the last of Rome-in-Britain. And beside him the beacon stack rose dark and waiting. . . . On a sudden wild impulse he flung open the bronze-sheathed chest in which the fire-lighting gear was kept, and pulled out flint and steel and tinderbox, and tearing his fingers on the steel in his frantic haste, as though he were fighting against time, he struck out fire and kindled the waiting tinder, and set about waking the beacon. Rutupiae Light should burn for this one more night. Maybe Felix or his old optio would know who had kindled it, but that was not what mattered. The pitch-soaked brushwood caught, and the flames ran crackling up, spreading into a great golden burst of fire; and the still, moonlit world below faded into a blue nothingness as the fierce glare flooded the beacon platform. The wind caught the crest of the blaze and bent it over in a wave; and Aquila's shadow streamed out from him across the parapet and into the night like a ragged cloak. He flung water from the tank in the corner on to the blackened bull's-hide fireshield, and crouched holding it before him by the brazier, feeding the blaze to its greatest strength. The heart of it was glowing now, a blasting, blinding core of heat and brightness under the flames; even from the shores of Gaul they would see the blaze, and say, 'Ah, there is Rutupiae's Light.' It was his farewell to so many things; to the whole world that he had been bred to. But it was something more: a defiance against the dark.

He vaguely, half expected them to come up from the town to see who had lit the beacon, but no one came. Perhaps they thought it was the ghosts. Presently he stoked it up so that it would last for a while, and turned to the stairhead and went clattering down. The beacon would sink low, but he did not think it would go out much before dawn.

He reached the ground level; the moonlight hung like a silver curtain before the doorway, and he walked out into it and across the deserted fortress, and out through a postern gate that stood open, and away. He had the sudden thought that for the sake of the fitness of things he should have broken his sword across his knee and left the pieces beside Rutupiae Light, but he was like to need it in the time that lay ahead.

1 Discuss Aquila's feelings here that led to his decision to light the beacon. Why was it 'a defiance against the dark'? Now imagine that you are Aquila. Describe your thoughts as you face life in a foreign country that you have chosen as your home, and what happens as you take up the challenge posed by your reason for making this choice that has altered the course of your life. (Afterwards, read Rosemary Sutcliff's novel and find out what did happen to Aquila, and the reason for his staying in Britain.) Why have you chosen to stay in Britain? Because of a girl whom you love? Because of a friend who needs your help? To settle a score with an enemy? To help the Britons in their fight against the Saxons? To remind them by your example of the light given them by Roman civilization, and to help maintain all the good things that Roman rule has brought them? Decide on what you imagine Aquila's motive for staying to be before you begin your story, and let it grow from there.

2 Imagine that you are one of Aquila's officer friends or an ordinary soldier in his command (perhaps you will choose

to be the Commandant Callistus, or the old man Aemilius who taught Aquila all he knows about being a soldier). Tell the story of what happened on board the 'Clytemnestra' when you discovered Aquila was 'wilful missing', and later saw the beacon blazing in the night sky. Describe your feelings about this, and your thoughts at leaving England for Rome.

3 Write a story that will show how important this Light was to the Romans. Perhaps you will imagine how and why it came to be built here (on the Kent coast) and what happened one night when someone failed to light it; or how it brought comfort to Roman sailors caught in a storm at sea far from their native land; the effect it had on the Britons when they first saw it alight; or an occasion when it blazed a message that troops inland had been dreading—the arrival of Saxon ships. . . .

4 Notice how the rhythm of the following poem is like that of the beam of a lighthouse going on and off 'over the land, over the sea':

Spurn Light

Punctually,
moment by moment, hour on hour, all night
punctually,
over the land, over the sea,
punctually,
moment by moment, hour on hour,
in its high tower,
punctually,
now dim, now bright,
the light
burns;
punctually,
moment by moment, hour on hour, all night,
over the land, over the sea,

punctually,
the light
turns.

It is the free
and wheeling gesture of a god: an arm
stretched to protect
the lonely cottage, and the farm
among its sleeping roofs asleep,
the dreaming village, and the old grey town,
where still one lighted window shows
a yellow square against the dark;
each little field and orchard-close,
the brown
and broken hedge, the stark
bare branches of the stooping tree,
and the waste place, by men forgot,
where, tumbled down,
the old house stands in the forlorn neglect
of what,
long since, had been a plot
of garden by the sea-winds wrecked. . . .

The far-flung arm
and gesture of a god,
stretched out over the grey main road
of the great estuary,
to keep
all those who go
by steam or canvas to and fro
between the river and the sea
from harm. . . .

An eye
that wakes for ever,
that takes the reach of all the river
and all the sea's horizons in its sweep. . . .

A star
that, when no other stars give light,

nor moon, in the black sky,
still winks through the bewildered night,
and by
its punctual eclipse
—moment by moment, hour on hour,
in its high tower—
sends its clear warning near and far
to all who pass in ships
on the great deep.

Punctually,
moment by moment, hour on hour,
now dim, now bright,
punctually,
the light
burns;
punctually,
moment by moment, hour on hour, all night,
over the land, over the sea,
punctually,
the light
turns.

                                    John Redwood Anderson

You are the keeper of this lighthouse. A violent storm
breaks down telephone communication between you and
the town, and your wireless is broken, because you have
fallen from a ladder on to it when inspecting a piece of
faulty mechanism in the light. Now, as you feared, the light
has stopped working. Will a ship crash on the rocks? Can
you repair your wireless? Will someone in the 'dreaming
village' or the 'grey town' have noticed and be on his way
with help? Describe what happens. *Or*, if you prefer,
imagine yourself to be the man in the photograph. It is your
watch. You have been looking for the light of the lighthouse
to guide you, but have seen nothing. You are beginning to
grow alarmed. . . .

5 Develop the following passage from *Lord of the Flies*—the story of a party of schoolboys whose plane (after an atomic war) has crashed on a tropical island:

Below the other side of the mountain-top was a platform of forest. Once more Ralph found himself making the cupping gesture.

'Down there we could get as much wood as we want.'

Jack nodded and pulled at his underlip. Starting perhaps a hundred feet below them on the steeper side of the mountain, the patch might have been designed expressly for fuel. Trees, forced by the damp heat, found too little soil for full growth, fell early and decayed: creepers cradled them, and new saplings searched a way up.

Jack turned to the choir, who stood ready. Their black caps of maintenance were slid over one ear like berets.

'We'll build a pile. Come on.'

They found the likeliest path down and began tugging at the dead wood. And the small boys who had reached the top came sliding too till everyone but Piggy was busy. Most of the wood was so rotten that when they pulled it broke up into a shower of fragments and woodlice and decay; but some trunks came out in one piece. The twins, Sam 'n Eric, were the first to get

90

a likely log but they could do nothing till Ralph, Jack, Simon, Roger and Maurice found room for a hand-hold. Then they inched the grotesque dead thing up the rock and toppled it over on top. Each party of boys added a quota, less or more, and the pile grew. At the return Ralph found himself alone on a limb with Jack and they grinned at each other, sharing this burden. Once more, amid the breeze, the shouting, the slanting sunlight on the high mountain, was shed that glamour, that strange invisible light of friendship, adventure, and content.

'Almost too heavy.'

Jack grinned back.

'Not for the two of us.'

Together, joined in effort by the burden, they staggered up the last steep of the mountain. Together, they chanted One! Two! Three! and crashed the log on to the great pile. Then they stepped back, laughing with triumphant pleasure, so that immediately Ralph had to stand on his head. Below them, boys were still labouring, though some of the small ones had lost interest and were searching this new forest for fruit. Now the twins, with unsuspected intelligence, came up the mountain with armfuls of dried leaves and dumped them against the pile. One by one, as they sensed that the pile was complete, the boys stopped going back for more and stood, with the pink, shattered top of the mountain around them. Breath came even by now, and sweat dried.

Ralph and Jack looked at each other while society paused about them. The shameful knowledge grew in them and they did not know how to begin confession.

Ralph spoke first, crimson in the face.

'Will you?'

He cleared his throat and went on.

'Will you light the fire?'

Now the absurd situation was open, Jack blushed too. He began to mutter vaguely.

'You rub two sticks. You rub—'

He glanced at Ralph, who blurted out the last confession of incompetence.

'Has anyone got any matches?'

'You make a bow and spin the arrow,' said Roger. He rubbed his hands in mime. 'Psss. Psss.'

A little air was moving over the mountain. Piggy came with it, in shorts and shirt, labouring cautiously out of the forest with the evening sunlight gleaming from his glasses. He held the conch under his arm.

Ralph shouted at him.

'Piggy! Have you got any matches?'

The other boys took up the cry till the mountain rang. Piggy shook his head and came to the pile.

'My! You've made a big heap, haven't you?'

Jack pointed suddenly.

'His specs—use them as burning glasses!'

Piggy was surrounded before he could back away.

'Here—let me go!' His voice rose to a shriek of terror as Jack snatched the glasses off his face. 'Mind out! Give 'em back! I can hardly see! You'll break the conch!'

Ralph elbowed him to one side and knelt by the pile.

'Stand out of the light.'

There was pushing and pulling and officious cries. Ralph moved the lenses back and forth, this way and that, till a glossy white image of the declining sun lay on a piece of rotten wood. Almost at once a thin trickle of smoke rose up and made him cough. Jack knelt too and blew gently, so that the smoke drifted away, thickening, and a tiny flame appeared. The flame, nearly invisible at first in that bright sunlight, enveloped a small twig, grew, was enriched with colour and reached up to a branch which exploded with a sharp crack. The flame flapped higher and the boys broke into a cheer.

'My specs!' howled Piggy. 'Give me my specs!'

Ralph stood away from the pile and put the glasses into Piggy's groping hands. His voice subsided to a mutter.

'Jus' blurs, that's all. Hardly see my hand—'

The boys were dancing. The pile was so rotten, and now so tinder-dry, that whole limbs yielded passionately to the yellow flames that poured upwards and shook a great beard of flame twenty feet in the air. For yards round the fire the heat was like a blow, and the breeze was a river of sparks. Trunks crumbled to white dust.

Ralph shouted.

'More wood! All of you get more wood!'

Life became a race with the fire and the boys scattered

through the upper forest. To keep a clean flag of flame flying on the mountain was the immediate end and no one looked further. Even the smallest boys, unless fruit claimed them, brought little pieces of wood and threw them in. The air moved a little faster and became a light wind, so that leeward and windward side were clearly differentiated. On one side the air was cool, but on the other the fire thrust out a savage arm of heat that crinkled hair on the instant. Boys who felt the evening wind on their damp faces paused to enjoy the freshness of it and then found they were exhausted. They flung themselves down in the shadows that lay among the shattered rocks. The beard of flame diminished quickly; then the pile fell inwards with a soft, cindery sound, and sent a great tree of sparks upwards that leaned away and drifted downwind. The boys lay, panting like dogs.

Ralph raised his head off his forearms.

'That was no good.'

Roger spat efficiently into the hot dust.

'What d'you mean?'

'There wasn't any smoke. Only flame.'

Piggy had settled himself into a coign between two rocks, and sat with the conch on his knees.

'We haven't made a fire,' he said, 'what's any use. We couldn't keep a fire like that going, not if we tried.'

'A fat lot you tried,' said Jack contemptuously. 'You just sat.'

'We used his specs,' said Simon, smearing a black cheek with his forearm. 'He helped that way.'

'I got the conch,' said Piggy indignantly. 'You let me speak!'

'The conch doesn't count on top of the mountain,' said Jack, 'so you shut up.'

'I got the conch in my hand.'

'Put on green branches,' said Maurice. 'That's the best way to make smoke.'

'I got the conch—'

Jack turned fiercely.

'You shut up!'

Piggy wilted. Ralph took the conch from him and looked round the circle of boys.

'We've got to have special people for looking after the fire. Any day there may be a ship out there'—he waved his arm at the taut wire of the horizon—'and if we have a signal going they'll come and take us off. And another thing. We ought to have more rules. Where the conch is, that's a meeting. The same up here as down there.'

They assented. Piggy opened his mouth to speak, caught Jack's eye and shut it again. Jack held out his hands for the conch and stood up, holding the delicate thing carefully in his sooty hands.

'I agree with Ralph. We've got to have rules and obey them. After all, we're not savages. We're English; and the English are best at everything. So we've got to do the right things.'

He turned to Ralph.

'Ralph—I'll split up the choir—my hunters, that is—into groups, and we'll be responsible for keeping the fire going.'

This generosity brought a spatter of applause from the boys, so that Jack grinned at them, then waved the conch at them for silence.

'We'll let the fire burn out now. Who would see smoke at night-time, anyway? And we can start the fire again whenever we like. Altos—you can keep the fire going this week; and trebles the next—'

The assembly assented gravely.

'And we'll be responsible for keeping a lookout too. If we see a ship out there'—they followed the direction of his bony arm with their eyes—'we'll put green branches on. Then there'll be more smoke.'

They gazed intently at the dense blue of the horizon, as if a little silhouette might appear there at any moment.

The sun in the west was a drop of burning gold that slid nearer and nearer the sill of the world. All at once they were aware of the evening as the end of light and warmth.

Roger took the conch and looked round at them gloomily.

'I've been watching the sea. There hasn't been the trace of a ship. Perhaps we'll never be rescued.'

A murmur rose and swept away. Ralph took back the conch.

'I said before we'll be rescued some time. We've just got to wait; that's all.'

Daring, indignant, Piggy took the conch.

'That's what I said! I said about our meetings and things and then you said shut up—'

His voice lifted into a whine of virtuous recrimination. They stirred and began to shout him down.

'You said you wanted a small fire and you been and built a pile like a hayrick. If I say anything,' cried Piggy, with bitter realism, 'you say shut up; but if Jack or Maurice or Simon—'

He paused in the tumult, standing, looking beyond them, and down at the unfriendly side of the mountain to the great patch where they had found dead wood. Then he laughed so strangely that they were hushed, looking at the flash of his spectacles in astonishment. They followed his gaze to find the sour joke.

'You got your small fire all right.'

Smoke was rising here and there among the creepers that

festooned the dead or dying trees. As they watched, a flash of fire appeared at the root of one wisp, and then the smoke thickened. Small flames stirred at the bole of a tree and crawled away through leaves and brushwood, dividing and increasing. One patch touched a tree trunk and scrambled up like a bright squirrel. The smoke increased, sifted, rolled outwards. The squirrel leapt on the wings of the wind and clung to another standing tree, eating downwards. Beneath the dark canopy of leaves and smoke the fire laid hold on the forest and began to gnaw. Acres of black and yellow smoke rolled steadily towards the sea. At the sight of the flames and the irresistible course of the fire, the boys broke into shrill, excited cheering. The flames, as though they were a kind of wild life, crept as a jaguar creeps on its belly towards a line of birch-like saplings that fledged an outcrop of the pink rock. They flapped at the first of the trees, and the branches grew a brief foliage of fire. The heart of flame leapt nimbly across the gap between the trees and then went swinging and flaring along the whole row of them. Beneath the capering boys a quarter of a mile square of forest was savage with smoke and flame. The separate noises of the fire merged into a drum-roll that seemed to shake the mountain.

'You got your small fire all right.'

Startled, Ralph realized that the boys were falling still and silent, feeling the beginnings of awe at the power set free below them.

William Golding

Look carefully at what Ralph says and does. What impressions have you formed of him as a leader? How does he compare with Jack? Do you find Jack's statement 'We've got to have rules and obey them. After all, we're not savages' surprising coming from his lips? What does Piggy feel about these other two boys, do you think? This is their second achievement so far since meeting and realizing what their situation is: their first was to elect Ralph as leader, because he blew the conch that called them all together. What impressions do you form of the boys' organizing ability from reading this extract? Discuss fully what emerges of the characters here before starting on

your story, and make sure that it develops the conflict between
Piggy, Ralph and Jack: remember that Jack is used to leading
his group of choir-school boys, and that some of the others are
as young as six years old.

Action

1 In groups read your versions of number **5** in the Composition section above, and select the most useful ideas from
   them as well as using the extract from *Lord of the Flies* for
   a play based on this event.
2 Prepare and rehearse the following poem for performance
   to the class:

Flannan Isle

'Though three men dwell on Flannan Isle
To keep the lamp alight,
As we steer'd under the lee, we caught
No glimmer through the night!'

A passing ship at dawn had brought
The news; and quickly we set sail,
To find out what strange thing might ail
The keepers of the deep-sea light.

The winter day broke blue and bright,
With glancing sun and glancing spray,
As o'er the swell our boat made way
As gallant as a gull in flight.

But, as we near'd the lonely Isle,
And look'd up at the naked height,
And saw the lighthouse towering white
With blinded lantern, that all night
Had never shot a spark
Of comfort through the dark,
So ghostly in the cold sunlight
It seem'd, that we were struck the while
With wonder all too dread for words.

And, as into the tiny creek
We stole beneath the hanging crag,
We saw three queer, black, ugly birds—
Too big, by far, in my belief,
For guillemot or shag—
Like seamen sitting bolt-upright
Upon a half-tide reef:
But, as we near'd, they plunged from sight,
Without a sound, or spurt of white.

And still too mazed to speak,
We landed; and made fast the boat;
And climb'd the track in single file,
Each wishing he were safe afloat,
On any sea, however far,
So be it far from Flannan Isle:
And still we seem'd to climb, and climb,
As though we'd lost all count of time,
And so must climb for evermore.
Yet, all too soon, we reached the door—

The black, sun-blister'd lighthouse-door,
That gaped for us ajar.

As, on the threshold, for a spell,
We paused, we seem'd to breathe the smell
Of limewash and of tar,
Familiar as our daily breath,
As though 'twere some strange scent of death:
And so, yet wondering, side by side,
We stood a moment, still tongue-tied:
And each with black foreboding eyed
The door, ere we should fling it wide,
To leave the sunlight for the gloom:
Till, plucking courage up, at last,
Hard on each other's heels we pass'd
Into the living-room.

Yet, as we crowded through the door,
We only saw a table, spread
For dinner, meat and cheese and bread;
But all untouch'd; and no one there:
As though, when they sat down to eat,
Ere they could even taste,
Alarm had come; and they in haste
Had risen and left the bread and meat:
For at the table-head a chair
Lay tumbled on the floor.
We listen'd; but we only heard
The feeble cheeping of a bird
That starved upon its perch:
And, listening still, without a word,
We set about our hopeless search.

We hunted high, we hunted low,
And soon ransack'd the empty house;
Then o'er the Island, to and fro,
We ranged, to listen and to look
In every cranny, cleft or nook
That might have hid a bird or mouse:
But, though we search'd from shore to shore,

We found no sign in any place:
And soon again stood face to face
Before the gaping door:
And stole into the room once more
As frighten'd children steal.

Ay: though we hunted high and low,
And hunted everywhere,
Of the three men's fate we found no trace
Of any kind in any place,
But a door ajar, and an untouch'd meal,
And an overtoppled chair.

And, as we listen'd in the gloom
Of that forsaken living-room—
A chill clutch on our breath—
We thought how ill-chance came to all
Who kept the Flannan Light:
And how the rock had been the death
Of many a likely lad:
How six had come to a sudden end,
And three had gone stark mad:
And one whom we'd all known as friend
Had leapt from the lantern one still night,
And fallen dead by the lighthouse wall:
And long we thought
On the three we sought,
And of what might yet befall.

Like curs a glance has brought to heel,
We listen'd flinching there:
And look'd, and look'd, on the untouch'd meal
And the overtoppled chair.

We seem'd to stand for an endless while,
Though still no word was said,
Three men alive on Flannan Isle
Who sought on three men dead.

Wilfrid Gibson

3 Now improvise a scene based on this poem, or add movement to the reading of the poem.
4 Write individual stories about what you think happened in the lighthouse to the three men (there is no need to explain *all* the mystery!). Read one another's versions and dramatize the best to add to what you developed in **3**.
5 Write a play based on the defeat of the Spanish Armada in 1588 and how terrified the ordinary English people had been of invasion by the Spaniards. The news of the defeat was sent from the south coast to London by the lights of beacons across the country. You are villagers. You see a fire lit in the distance and the truth dawns on you. Now it is your duty to pass the joyful news on. . . .

C London's burning

Use the following material to build up a documentary drama about the Great Fire of London of 1666.

Action

SEPTEMBER 1ST

Scene 1   A bakery in Pudding Lane

1 Thomas Farynor, the king's baker, and his daughter, Hannah, are woken by thick smoke: the wood used to light their oven has caught fire. They think they are trapped.
2 With the help of their servants they climb up on to the roof and let themselves down next door—all, that is, except the maid, who falls back into the flames.

Scene 2   The Guildhall

3 Someone rushes to the guard to tell him of the danger. A wind has risen and already carried the fire to the stables of the Star Inn: the burning straw has in turn set the Inn ablaze. Nearby are warehouses stocked with tar, oil, brandy. . . . The Mayor must be woken and told.

4 The Mayor is woken: he drank too much earlier this night and says there is nothing to fear.

Scene 3   Samuel Pepys's house

5 Samuel Pepys goes to bed. His servants have to stay up to prepare for a party he is going to give tomorrow. Imagine their feelings about having to work while their master sleeps and their conversation about the coming day. Find out what foods they will be preparing.

6 One of the servants notices a strange brightness in the sky. She goes to Jane's bedroom window and discovers there is a fire burning in the City of London. Should the servants wake their master? Jane decides she'd better.

7 Samuel Pepys's reaction was described in his diary:

'Jane called us up to tell us of a great fire they saw in the City. So I rose and slipped on my nightgown, and went to her window; I thought it far enough off, and so went to bed again, and to sleep.'

8 How do his servants react to this?

Scenes 4 and 5

9 Scenes to show the spreading of the fire:

    a the Lord Mayor organizes a team of men with leathern buckets. Too late—the fire has reached the warehouses and the houses on London Bridge.

    b he orders men to get firehooks from the churches (where they are kept) to pull down the wooden houses with their thatched roofs. Why? He is still too late.

Scene 6

10 Samuel Pepys realizes that the Lord Mayor is powerless and visits King Charles II, who orders him to tell the Lord Mayor to pull down any building in the path of the fire. Pepys wrote in his diary:

    'About four o'clock in the morning my Lady Batten sent me a cart to carry away all my money and plate, and best things, which I did, riding myself in my nightgown, in the cart; and Lord! to see how the streets and highways are crowded with people running and riding.'

Perhaps he will tell the King about this during their conversation.

Scenes 7–?

11 People panic to get out of the town. Rumours spread. Who started it? The Dutch, say some. Roman Catholics, say others (find out why these should be accused). City merchants even accuse the King, because they think he fears their getting too much power. Foreigners have been seen throwing firebombs into buildings. Religious maniacs scream that the end of the world is nigh, and swear that they prophesied it would come like this.

12 The Duke of York is put in control. The troops are brought in to organize local inhabitants in pulling down houses (pay = £5 worth of bread and cheese and beer). But they can't get them down quickly enough, and are forced to use gunpowder. The rich merchants try to stop them destroying their fine houses. The King rides about encouraging them, holding a bag of £100 in coin, giving a sovereign to anyone he sees working especially hard, and helps in the human chains pouring the buckets of water on the flames, and with the fire-pump.

Composition

Write eye-witness accounts of the fire from various people's points of view, for example: **a** Thomas Farynor **b** his daughter **c** Pepys's servant, Jane **d** the Lord Mayor **e** a merchant **f** a soldier **g** a criminal released from the Debtors' Prison just in time. . . .

Here are some more:

John Evelyn
The statues of Paul's flew like grenades, the melting lead running down the streets in a stream, and the very pavements glowing with fiery redness, so as no horse, nor man, was able to tread on them, and the demolition had stopped all passages, so that no help could be applied. . . .

Henry Griffith
(The firefighters) rode up and down, giving orders for blowing up of houses with gunpowder, to make void spaces for the fire to die in, and standing still to see those orders executed, exposing their persons not only to the multitude, but to the very flames themselves, and the ruins of the buildings ready to fall upon them, and sometimes labouring with their own hands to give example to others: for which the people now do pay them, as they ought to do, all possible reverence and admiration.

William Tanswell
But what rendered our loss still greater was this: certain persons, assuming the characters of porters, but in reality nothing else but downright plunderers, came and offered their assistance in removing our goods. We accepted: but they so far availed themselves of our service as to steal goods to the value of £40 from us.

The Reverend Thomas Vincent
Rattle, rattle, rattle, was the noise which the Fire struck . . . as if there had been 1000 iron chariots beating upon the stones;

and if you opened your eyes to the opening of the streets, where the Fire was come, you might see in some places whole streets at once in flames, that issued forth, as if they had been so many great forges from the opposite windows, which folding together were united together in one great flame throughout the whole street, and then you might see the houses tumble, tumble, tumble, from one end of the street to the other with a great crash, leaving the foundations open to the ocean of the heavens. . . .

Many thousands now have nowhere to lay their heads, and the fields are the only receptacle where they can find for themselves and their goods; most of the late inhabitants of London be all night in the open air, with no other canopy over them, but that of the Heavens.

Intersperse the scenes you have worked out with readings from these accounts and from the best of those you have imagined.

Action

End your play with the trial of the scapegoat—Hubert, a 25-year-old French watchmaker.

1 There is no defence: he confesses, saying that he had been plotting abroad for a year, and has been able to point out the exact spot in the bakery where the fire started. He threw a fireball through a window. But even Thomas and Hannah Farynor (why have I written 'even'?) swear that there was no window for him to throw his fireball through.

2 The procession through the streets—remember that there will be hundreds of homeless, starving people glad of the chance of revenge on this foreigner. He is hanged at Tyburn.

3 The captain of the Swedish ship on which Hubert travelled to England swears to Lord Clarendon on oath that his ship did not reach England until two days after the fire had begun. Why has he not revealed this earlier?

4 Lord Clarendon's reaction was:

'Neither the judges nor any present at the trial did believe him guilty, but that he was a poor distracted wretch weary of his life, and chose to part with it in this way!'

5 What would other people's reactions have been? End your drama on their final thoughts as they look at their ruined homes and city. And what other (perhaps even more terrible) catastrophe haunts their memory from the year before?

4 Flood

A Storm

I

Against the stone breakwater,
Only an ominous lapping,
While the wind whines overhead,
Coming down from the mountain,
Whistling between the arbours, the winding terraces;

A thin whine of wires, a rattling and flapping of leaves,
And the small streetlamp swinging and slamming against the
  lamp-pole.
Where have the people gone?
There is one light on the mountain.

II

Along the sea-wall a steady sloshing of the swell,
The waves not yet high, but even,
Coming closer and closer upon each other;
A fine fume of rain driving in from the sea,
Riddling the sand, like a wide spray of buckshot,
The wind from the sea and the wind from the mountain con-
  tending,
Flicking the foam from the whitecaps straight upwards into the
  darkness.

A time to go home!
And a child's dirty shift billows upward out of an alley;
A cat runs from the wind as we do,
Between the whitening trees, up Santa Lucia,
Where the heavy door unlocks
And our breath comes more easy.
Then a crack of thunder, and the black rain runs over us, over
The flat-roofed houses, coming down in gusts, beating
The walls, the slatted windows, driving
The last watcher indoors, moving the cardplayers closer
To their cards, their Lachryma Christi.

III

We creep to our bed and its straw mattress.
We wait, we listen.
The storm lulls off, then redoubles,
Bending the trees halfway down to the ground,
Shaking loose the last wizened oranges in the orchard,
Flattening the limber carnations.
A spider eases himself down from a swaying light bulb,
Running over the coverlet, down under the iron bedstead.

110

The bulb goes on and off, weakly.
Water roars in the cistern.

We lie closer on the gritty pillow,
Breathing heavily, hoping—
For the great last leap of the wave over the breakwater,
The flat boom on the beach of the towering sea-swell,
The sudden shudder as the jutting sea-cliff collapses
And the hurricane drives the dead straw into the living pine-
    trees.

                                        Theodore Roethke

Discussion

1 Discuss how the poet makes us feel the storm rising, step by step.

2 Why does he look at the storm from the point of view of a man and his wife sheltering from it? What do the details of where they are and what they do contribute to our understanding of it?

3 Study the ways in which the sounds of the storm are conveyed to us.

4 Look carefully at the small details which make this experience seem frightening and ominous.

5 Discuss the effects of these lines:
'A thin whine of wires, a rattling and flapping of leaves'
'And a child's dirty shift billows upward out of an alley'
'A spider eases himself down from a swaying light bulb'
'Breathing heavily, hoping—
For the great last leap of the wave over the breakwater . . .'
—why 'hoping' here? Which other lines did you find particularly effective? Why?

6 Tell one another of storms that you particularly remember: perhaps when you were caught by one, a long way from shelter, or when you were at home, watching it through the window (or hiding from it!).

7 Why are people frightened of thunderstorms? What is the danger in them?

8 Find out exactly what causes storms and explain them to the class or group—and about hurricanes, tornadoes, and other violent storms in other countries.

9 How do changes in the weather affect animals—fish, for instance? Tell one another what you have noticed.

10 Think about how the foreboding sense of a storm is gradually built up in the atmosphere, and the effects on sky, trees and flowers, animals, ourselves: make up a group oral word-picture of the scene for the others to listen to. You may wish to add percussion to help point the changes you are describing.

Composition

1 Now describe the storm you remember most vividly, stage by stage. Perhaps you will imagine a person or people being frightened by it and describe the storm mainly through its effects on them, as Theodore Roethke has done (notice that he doesn't actually *tell* us explicitly that they are frightened, but builds up a picture of their fear through physical details), or on yourself, or on an animal. Try to choose an individual viewpoint.

2 Make in groups a sound-poem of a storm. First think of the description you made in groups, and then concentrate on finding as many individual words and sounds as you can that will, through the noises made when speaking them, convey the gradual development of the storm. Work out which words will be repeated and build up a rhythm that will correspond to a storm's (use the percussion noises you may have worked out already, too). Tape your poem so that you can hear for yourselves if the ideas work, then rehearse and perform it to the rest of the class.

3 Read one another's descriptions written in **1** above, then build up a group poem that describes a storm entirely visually, in word-pictures, arranging images selected from your individual pieces of writing into a new pattern.

4 Now blend the two group poems and rehearse them for presentation to the class, perhaps adding movement. Discuss the difference between what you did first in the Discussion section above and this performance.

5 Write a story about being lost in a storm or blizzard.

6 Write about someone who has to go out in the storm because he has no choice, for instance a shepherd, a policeman, an escaped convict, a member of a mountain rescue
team. Or write about a hungry animal searching for food
and the effects of the storm on this creature.

7 Choose one of the photographs included in this section as
the basis for a poem or story.

8 Watch rain sliding down the window pane: follow the path
of each rain-drop, note the patterns they form. Write about
the thoughts that they bring to your mind.

9 Write accurate descriptions in note form of
  a the touch of rain, mist or fog, snow or sleet, hail, the wind on your skin
  b the sounds they make
  c the way they change your view of the buildings and streets around you
  d the way other people react to contact with them, both physically when outside and in what they say and do when they come indoors
  e how the scene is changed after the items listed in **a** have ceased.
10 Build your notes into extended descriptions or poems as

detailed as the following poem by Edward Thomas, where he writes about a day of heavy rain, piecing his description together like a jigsaw. How would you describe the mood of this poem? How does it differ from the other poem in this section? What is added to the words by the poem's peculiar movement, with its long and short lines?

After Rain

The rain of a night and a day and a night
Stops at the light
Of this pale choked day. The peering sun
Sees what has been done.
The road under the trees has a border new
Of purple hue
Inside the border of bright thin grass:
For all that has
Been left by November of leaves is torn
From hazel and thorn
And the greater trees. Throughout the copse
No dead leaf drops
On grey grass, green moss, burnt-orange fern,
At the wind's return;
The leaflets out of the ash-tree shed
Are thinly spread
In the road, like little black fish, inlaid
As if they played.
What hangs from the myriad branches down there
So hard and bare
Is twelve yellow apples lovely to see
On one crab tree.
And on each twig of every drop in the dell
Uncountable
Crystals both dark and bright of the rain
That begins again.

Collect your best pieces together for a class anthology, perhaps illustrated by your paintings of similar scenes to those described in your poems.

B Storm at sea

Then the storm—which had lain in wait for us like a wild beast—sprang. They say that a storm at sea is the most terrifying of all disasters. And so it is. If I hadn't been mortally seasick all the while, I'd surely died of fright. Waves turned to rock and thundered on our sides to be let in, while icy water poured down through our upper seams—though which was upper and which was lower in that dark a shipwright would have been hard put to know: for I'll swear there were whole minutes when the *Charming Molly* showed her very keel to heaven!

For a good half of the tempest, my stomach must have thrown up every meal I'd had in my life: for a worse half, I prayed for I don't know what: and for the worst half of all (a storm cares nothing for arithmetic and has as many halves as it chooses) I lay nearly dead of a blow from that thankless sack I'd freed to make me a pillow.

When I came to myself again, I was wet and weak and aching both inside and out. The motion of the ship had subsided and I thought God had grown less angry with the world. I heard steps above me once more, and the sailors singing again.

'There she goes,' I heard the captain say, 'like a great black tiger in the sky. D'you see her, mister? Long tail and a great paw dripping down into the sea? Murdering beast!' The storm had passed us by.

We continued on our way for an hour or more, during which time I brooded on how best to make myself known to the captain and crew. I'd recovered enough to be hungry and thirsty, and I longed for a sight of the sea and sky. Though I'd little enough to tell, the way of saying it somehow stuck in my throat. With no name but that of a parish, I was a poor addition to any ship's company. So I thought awhile on my vanished mother and wondered if she still lived. This was not a new thought, for many a time at the cobbler's it had come . . .

I used to fancy myself to be of noble blood, snatched for some dark cause, and would look—sonlike—at such elegant ladies who called. Some smiled, some complained, but none looked back motherlike. I thought I had a birthmark once, just above my knee: but it wore away with too much washing—as did the fondest of my dreams. I'd never have abandoned the cobbler if those dreams hadn't abandoned me first.

Still, somewhere I'd had a mother, and that was for certain-sure, and wherever in the world she was, I asked her now for her blessing on her forgotten son's enterprise. In another minute, I'd have got my courage and gone up on deck. But I waited for that minute in which I was most surely blessed.

A confused shouting broke out above. Men began running violently across the deck with feet like thunder. A ship had been sighted away to the starboard bow. It seemed she was not above half a mile off and sorely torn by the storm. Her masts were snapped and her rigging carried off, and she was desperately low in the water. She was flying no flag—there was nothing left to fly one from. But good or bad, English or otherwise, it was plain to the sailors above she was not long for this world.

The captain's harsh voice drove the men from pity to action and I felt us tilt sharply as we changed course to starboard. I heard the crack of rope against canvas, which can sometimes be as sharp as musket-fire; and I heard the grunt of sails as they took the wind and we leaped forward joyously on our errand of mercy.

Then our canvas was hauled in and our pace began to drop as we drew close. Presently I could hear the sea slopping the sides of that other vessel in a weary kind of way, as if to say, 'I've done with you. Why don't you go to the bottom?' Then I heard grappling ropes flung from ship to ship and made fast. I heard men clambering aboard: fifteen, twenty, even thirty I counted before I began to think there was something amiss.

For none of them spoke a word. Just the thud-thud as their feet landed on the deck, then nothing. Had they been so battered and beaten by the storm that they'd lost the power of thanks, or speech?

A great uneasiness seemed to lie on the ship, and the men of the *Charming Molly* fell as silent as the strangers. It was a very bitter stillness as half a hundred hearts grew cold when they saw what they'd rescued.

'Well, for God's sake!' shouted a single voice—

By way of answer there came a crackling, spiteful roar as between thirty and forty muskets and pistols were discharged into the bellies, brains, hearts and lungs of the rescuers. A great many fell at once, in a clumsy, lumpish manner, tumbling among legs and feet not quick enough to avoid them. Then those who were not hit began running in a despairing kind of way, scudding from side to side, hopping on a turn, till too great a hurry brought its own calamitous reward.

At the beginning, there was a tremendous amount of screaming and shouting and raging to God: then this got less as the need diminished and the murdered sailors understood there was to be nothing for them but despatch. A few remaining voices cried out women's names with melancholy affection till a loud, full period was put to them, too. Five or six pistol shots concluded the whole, each being followed by its customary grunt of collapse.

A remarkable lad would have gone up in the midst of all this and maybe survived to tell the tale. Maybe. He would have fought with teeth and nails and feet and done some damage before he was stopped.

A less remarkable lad stayed where he was, nine parts out of his mind with terror—and the tenth, wishing himself anywhere else in the world. Every patch of wet his hands slipped into, he conceived to be blood: though it's certain very little dripped through from the deck into the hold. Indeed, the leaking remains were very quickly posted into the sea—sometimes two and three at a time, so it was hard to say how many there had once been.

I think maybe forty, of whom not one, not one! I understood to've survived this last calamity that came out of the storm. The ship had been taken by pirates.

Leon Garfield

Discussion and Composition

1 Discuss the impressions you have formed of the narrator in this passage. Why, do you think, has he become a stowaway? How would you feel if you were in his position? From what you have gathered of his character here, how do

you imagine he will confront the danger that now awaits him?

2 Imagine that you are the boy telling this story. Continue it in the way you imagine he would.

3 Read one another's versions and decide which is the most likely development, as regards both the story and your impressions of the boy's character. Are the styles used by other members of the group similar to that of the extract (from a novel called *Jack Holborn*)? Does the same voice seem to be speaking in each case? Obtain a copy of this novel if you can and compare its development of this situation with yours. Then read the whole story.

4 Listen to Benjamin Britten's 'Sea Interludes' from *Peter Grimes*, particularly the section describing a storm at sea:
  a write a poem about what the music brings to your mind
  b in groups, either i without using any furniture or props make yourselves become sailors fighting the storm that is attacking your ship, or ii make a dance drama of the storm in which some of you are the sea and storm, and others the ships that are battered by them.
  c The music could now accompany the movement while a few of the poems are read aloud.

5 Write a story based on the following poem:

The Singing Sailor

The sea was fifty miles away
Sliding beneath the moon;
Far was the inn upon the shore
And the nautical tune.

I walked a solitary road
And did not hear a sound
Apart from steps that were my own
Falling upon the ground.

A great tree twisted to the sky
(Here a robber's corpse could hang)
And as I passed that silent tree
The singing sailor sang.

I passed the tree, and heard no more
The singing sailor's tune.
The road looked like a curl of smoke
In the light of the moon.

Clifford Dyment

Who is the 'singing sailor'? What voice can be heard from
the 'silent tree' at night? Let your story explain the mystery
of his identity, the terrible truth that lies behind the 'great
tree twisted to the sky'. One way of approaching this story
would be to describe in detail the scene of the poem. You
return to the lonely cottage where you are staying, looking
back on the road that looks 'like a curl of smoke' and re-
membering the stories told of 'the singing sailor' at the inn.
You try to dismiss your thoughts as being mere idle fancies.
You go to bed—but you can't sleep. You switch on the
light and take a book from the shelf by your bed: it is called
'The Singing Sailor'. What you read fills you with dread.
Your hair stands on end as you recall that 'great tree
twisted to the sky' that you saw when you paused in the

moonlight two hours ago. Suddenly the silence is broken by a low, steady tapping on the window downstairs. . . .

6 Read your stories to one another in as mysterious and chilling a manner as you can. Then choose the best (or extracts from the best) for a group reading to the class, also rehearsing and reading the poem that started them.

7 Use the photographs that illustrate this section as illustrations to a story. Perhaps there is a bad storm at night. A ship is wrecked on the treacherous rocks out at sea where many ships have perished in the past. You are a member of the lifeboat team. In dangerous seas you hunt for survivors. There seem to be none. Then you glimpse something that puts you on the alert—three men on a piece of driftwood, their arms outstretched. Quickly you tell the rest of the crew to alter course. But the men have disappeared and you cannot find them . . . and three men were washed overboard in a storm exactly a year ago to-night . . . washed overboard from this lifeboat on which you are standing. . . .

8 Here is another disturbing poem. Read it carefully and then discuss what you think lies behind it:

Nelson Gardens

As I was walking in Nelson Gardens
A stroppy young seaman came my way,
He put his candid hand in mine
And these were the words I heard him say:

Come with me where the winking waters
Beam as bright as washing-day,
And Old Man Neptune's darling daughters
Round their father's garden play.

Buckle your belt with a Lincoln dollar,

THE
PUNCH
BOWL
INN

A.D.1638

Turn your money and make a wish,
The world will touch your lucky collar,
Jump in your pocket like a flying-fish.

Come with me where the briny billow
Is sweet as the grass upon the hill,
The sun will smooth your single pillow
And the terrible tongue of the clock is still.

Off I went with the easy sailor,
But the truth was hard as stone:
Though we sail the seas together
Each of us must sail alone.

Bitter was the brilliant water,
Ever faster spoke the clock,
And the palace was a prison,
And the pillow was a rock.

Early in the morning when the sun was rising
Up came the moon all rosy-red,
Blew the stars out of the heaven,
Spiked the sky on our mast-head.

By my side I saw my comrade
Freezing in the noonday heat,
And his suit was made of canvas
A lump of lead was at his feet.

Now my hair is white as paper,
Thin my finger as the pen,
As the weather from the winter
Turns to summer once again.

As I was walking in Nelson Gardens
A stroppy young seaman came my way,
He put his candid hand in mine
And these were the words I heard him say.

                                    Charles Causley

a What is meant by 'the terrible tongue of the clock is still'? How is this line echoed later?

b Why does Charles Causley write
Though we sail the seas together
Each of us must sail alone?

c Describe carefully what you think happens in the seventh stanza. What is the effect of 'spiked' on you when you read it? Why has the poet used this word here?

d Explain what you feel the connection is between the seventh stanza and the eighth.

e Why is the last stanza a repetition of the first?

9 Write a long story (even a novel) based on what you feel lies behind this poem: use extracts from the poem as chapter headings.

10 Read one another's stories, then use the best as the basis for an improvised play, with the author as director. Alternatively, you may prefer to write in pairs a play based on one of the stories you have written—or even merge the best ideas of both stories to form a new plot for your script.

C The great flood

Many ancient literatures point to a great flood sent by God to punish mankind for its wickedness—a storm to end all storms. Here is the ancient Greek version:

There was such wickedness once on earth that Justice fled to the sky, and the king of the gods determined to make an end of the race of men. Then Jupiter let loose the South Wind, and the South Wind came with drenching wings. He veiled his terrible face in pitchy darkness; his beard was heavy with the storm and his hair was streaked grey with rain. Clouds sat upon his forehead; water poured from his feathers and the folds of his garments. He squeezed in his fist the hanging masses of cloud, and there was a crash. Thick vapours fell from the air, and Iris, the messenger of Juno, dressed in rainbow colours, carried water to feed the clouds.

The crops were battered to the ground and farmers wept for their fallen hopes; for all the year's work had turned out to have been useless.

Jupiter's anger was not confined to his province of the sky. Neptune, his sea-blue brother, sent the waves to help him. He summoned the rivers and when they had entered the palace of their lord, he said: 'No need for many words. Just pour out the whole of your strength. That is what I want. Open all your doors, let nothing stop you, but give free rein to your flowing streams!' So he commanded, and they went away. Then the springs ran unchecked and the rivers rolled unbridled to the seas. Neptune smote the earth with his trident and the earth shivered and shook, giving free passage to the waters under the

earth. The rivers broke their bounds and went rushing over the lowlands, dragging along with them fields of corn and orchards, men and beasts together, houses and religious buildings with all their holy images. If there was any house left which could stand up against the flood without crashing down, yet its roof was under water and its turrets were hid by the waves eddying above. Soon there was no telling land from sea. The whole world was sea, except that this sea had no shores.

You could see the men, one getting up on to a hill, another sitting in his curved boat, using oars now in the very place where he had been ploughing only a moment before. Another man is sailing over corn fields or over the roof of some great submerged house; yet another is catching fish among the topmost boughs of an elm. Perhaps their anchors grapple the green grass of meadows, or the curved keels scrape over vines growing under water. And where the light-limbed goats used to crop the turf, now ugly-looking seals go flopping about.

Under the water the sea-nymphs Nereides are staring in amazement at woods, houses and cities. The forests are now full of dolphins who dash about in the tops of the trees and beat their tails against the swaying trunks. You might see a wolf swimming with a flock of sheep, yellow lions carried away by the water, and tigers too. The wild boar, though he is strong as a thunderbolt, cannot help himself, nor is the stag's fleet foot any use to him. He too is swept away; and the birds, after they have wandered far and looked everywhere for a place to alight, fall into the sea too weak to move their wings.

The sea, in its boundless power, had flattened out the smaller hills, and waves, never seen there before, were lapping round the crests of mountains. Nearly all the men perished by water; and those who escaped the water, having no food, died of hunger.

Composition

1 Imagine yourself to be one of the victims of the flood. Imagine this disaster is happening now. Describe what you see and think, using the information given in this passage, and imagining further details of your own.

2 Now read the rest of the story below, then imagine yourself to be either Deucalion or Pyrrha; re-tell the story as it happened to you.

There is a place called Phocis, a rich land, while there was any land, but at that time it was part of the sea, just a huge plain of hurrying water. There is a mountain there whose twin peaks seem to aim at the stars. It is called Parnassus and its summit is above the clouds. All the country round was under water, but Deucalion with his wife, in a little boat, got to this mountain and landed. There was no man more good or more devoted to fair dealing than Deucalion, and there was no more reverent woman than his wife, Pyrrha.

Now when Jupiter saw that the whole earth had become one lake of running water, and that from so many thousands of men and women only this one man and this one woman were left, and that both of them were innocent, both good decent folk, then he dispersed the clouds, made the north wind roll away the rain, and unveiled again the whole vault of heaven. The sea no longer raged. The ruler of the deep laid aside his three-pronged spear and calmed the waters. He called for sea-blue Triton and soon Triton's head rose out of the deep and his shoulders all overgrown with barnacles. Neptune told him to blow on his horn of shell the signal for retreat to waves and rivers. He took up his bugle, a spiral shell, twisted at the mouthpiece and opening out wide at the other end. When he draws in his breath and blows into this bugle the sound goes out from the middle of the sea to the ends of the world. So now as soon as the shell had touched the lips and dripping beard of the god and the blast had been blown calling the retreat, the sound was heard by all the waters of earth and sea, and they obeyed, one and all. Now the sea has shores again, streams run brimming their channels, rivers go back to their beds, and the hills begin to appear. The earth emerges; land grows as water shrinks away, and as time passes woods appear below the naked summits of the hills, though mud still sticks to the leaves of the trees.

So the world came back again. But when Deucalion saw it all empty, and all the countries lying desolate in a tremendous silence, tears came into his eyes and he spoke thus to Pyrrha:

'My sister, my wife, you, the only woman left, once it was our family, our birth and our wedding that brought us together, but now our dangers are another bond. We two are all the inhabitants of all the lands that the sun looks on when it rises and when it sets. The sea has the rest. And even now we cannot be sure that we are safe. The terror of those clouds still sticks in my mind. Poor creature, what would you feel like now, if you had been preserved from fate without me? How would you endure terror, if you were alone? Who then would be trying to console you? As for me I am sure that if you had been drowned I should go after you and be drowned too. Oh how I wish that I had the skill of Prometheus, my father, and could get all the people back again and pour life into moulded clay! As it is the whole race of mankind is comprised in us two, and we seem to have been preserved just as specimens of humanity. Such was the will of heaven.'

So he spoke, weeping, and then they decided to pray to the powers above, and ask for help from the holy oracle. Together they went straight away to the waters of Cepheus, which were not yet running clear, but they knew where the shallows were and so passed through them. They took water from the stream and sprinkled it on their heads and garments; then they went to the shrine of the holy goddess and saw the roof of the shrine shining with foul sea-slime, and the altars with no fire burning on them. When they reached the steps of the temple, they both fell on their faces and reverently kissed the ice-cold stones. Then they spoke: 'If the powers of heaven can feel anything or be at all moved by the prayers of the just, if the anger of the gods is not inflexible, then tell us, O Themis, what skill there is by which we can repair the ruin of the race. Lend thine aid, O most merciful one, to the drowned!'

Moved with compassion, the goddess gave her answer: 'Go forth from the temple. Veil your heads and unloose the girdles of your garments. Then scatter behind you on the ground the bones of your venerable mother.'

For a long time they stood still in amazement, till Pyrrha first broke the silence, and said that she could not do what the goddess had bidden them. Her lips trembled as she begged for pardon; but how could she dare to wound her mother's ghost by throwing her bones about? All the time they pondered within themselves and revolved in their minds the difficult words of the goddess's reply, so dark to understand.

Finally Deucalion found soothing words to calm his wife. 'Oracles,' he said, 'are good things and could never tell us to do anything bad. Now, either my usual intelligence has gone astray, or else "our venerable mother" is the earth. And by "bones" I think the oracle must mean the stones that are in the body of the earth. It is stones that we are told to scatter behind us.'

Pyrrha was certainly impressed by her husband's interpretation, but still they hardly dared to hope. So mistrustful were they both of the commands of heaven. Still there was no harm in trying, so they went out of the temple, veiled their heads, girded up their tunics, and, as they had been told, scattered stones behind them as they went. Antiquity is our evidence for what happened next. Otherwise I doubt whether anyone would believe it. For the stones began to lose their hardness. Little by little they grew soft, and as they softened they began to take a new shape. They went on growing; something less hard than stone was stirring within them, something like humanity, although it was not quite clear yet, but more like pieces of sculpture that have only just been begun, which are more or less like what they are meant to be, but are not yet quite rounded off. All the earth and mud which stick to the stones became flesh; the solid core became bones; veins in the mineral were still veins, but now they had blood in them. And in a short time, by the power of the gods, all the stones which Deucalion had sown grew up into men, and women sprang from the stones which Pyrrha scattered.

So we human beings are a hard stubborn race, well used to labour; and that is how we prove that this story of our birth is true.

Translated by Rex Warner

Action

Prepare a dramatized reading of this story:

a Build up (first in groups and later as a class) a script based on extracts from the text printed here and from the best eye-witness accounts you yourselves have written.

b Rehearse your scripts, making them sound as dramatic as possible.

c Now pay attention to the visual impact of your reading. Will you always stand in the same place? When would it be effective for you to move? Can you use rostra to give different levels?

d Are there occasions when background music will help? If so, tape it, or rehearse your own.

e Add movement, first for Deucalion and Pyrrha, then symbolic movement to help express the different stages of the action: the devastation caused by the flood/the falling away of the sea/the growth of stones into people.

Polish your production for performance to another class.

Research

1 In a Bible, read Genesis Chapter 6, beginning at verse 5 'And God saw that the wickedness of man was great in the Earth. . . .' and continue to verse 17 of Chapter 9.

2 Read also, if you can, *The Log of the Ark* by Kenneth Walker and Geoffrey Boumphrey (a lot of which is very amusing) and the play *Noah* by André Obey. Discuss what these very different versions of the same story have added to the original. What has caught the imagination of the writers?

3 Find out about the Medieval Gilds and the Mystery Plays they performed at religious festivals. How did they stage these plays? Who wrote them? Which gild would have produced the story of Noah, and why?

Action

Make up your own play of the story of Noah, using some or all of the characters listed in Genesis.

1 How will you make these characters different from one

another? The medieval plays make great fun of Noah's wife, making her into a nagging gossip who refuses to believe Noah and leads the other wives in a revolt against the men, which is only stopped by brute force. Use your imagination to make the other characters interesting also.

2 How will the wives differ from one another and from Noah's wife? Discuss their characters fully and then test them in a situation, for instance complaining about the faults of their husbands.

3 Use your imagination to make interesting conflicts between the brothers also. How will their characters differ from each other and from Noah? See if you have established them clearly by improvising the scene in which Noah tells his sons what God has told him. How will they react? Will they all be convinced immediately? The girls in the group can watch the boys' version when they have worked it out, and see if it is convincing. Give constructive criticism on how the scene could be improved, especially thinking of how the characters can be drawn more clearly. Do the different characters come across clearly in action? Do they walk, speak, sit in character? Is enough made of the possible tensions (and fun) in the conflicts that are possible between them? Watch very closely and then give clear advice on how the acting could be improved.

4 Now it is the girls' turn (or you could work out and practise your scene while the boys are preparing theirs). Imagine the scene when Noah's wife comes to tell you of his ridiculous notion that he has got into his head. The boys in the group can now watch the girls' scene and offer criticism in the same way as they have done.

5 Work again on your scenes, using the criticisms you have heard to make them more interesting and convincing. Then show them to each other again.

6 Now bring the boys and girls in the group together in a scene in which Noah and his sons try to convince their wives of the truth. They fail. Now add the following scenes:

7 Noah and his sons construct their Ark. Use no props—but

really concentrate on imagining the tools and planks, etc., as if they really are in your hands: their size, weight, shape and texture. It will probably be necessary for you to work on this vital aspect first before working out the scene: practise handling imaginary tools and lengths of wood, first by yourself and then passing them to each other (a useful preliminary exercise would be to pass a chair from one member of the group to the next, concentrating on trying to remember exactly what its weight and size are like and how you take hold of it, lift it and let go of it—and then pretend that you are passing the same chair around in exactly the same way). Establish clearly the final size and shape of the Ark in your minds, so that you can each visualize its existence. Now join in building the Ark in the space before you.

8 The women watch the men's work with scorn and make rude remarks about it. They try to sabotage the men's efforts—but fail, and leave them to it, and go away to enjoy themselves.

9 The first rain falls. The men must hurry. The pairs of animals must be rounded up and got on board. The situation is urgent. The women continue to jeer and scoff. At last all the animals are on board (imagine these with the same care as you imagined the Ark and the building of it). The water is rising fast. The women refuse to come on board. Noah and the men argue with the women, plead, threaten. Finally the women give in, but Noah's wife holds out to the last and the other women have to join the men in dragging her on board.

10 Decide on which scenes should follow to complete the story and improvise them.

Research

When you have worked out your complete play, try to find a medieval version and compare it with yours. Here is an extract from one. You may like to act it.

NOAH	Now are we there, as we should be;
	Go, get in our gear, cattle and company,
	Into this vessel here, my children free.
WIFE	Shut up was I never, so God save me,
	In such an oyster as this.
	In faith I cannot find
	Which is before, which is behind;
	Shall we here be confined,
	Noah, as have thou bliss?

NOAH	Dame, peace and still, we must abide grace;
	Therefore, wife, with good will, come into this place.
WIFE	Sir, for Jack nor for Gill, will I turn my face,
	Till I have on this hill, spun a space
	On my distaff;
	Woe to him who moves me,
	Now will I down set me,
	And let no man prevent me,
	For him will I strafe.

NOAH	Behold in the heaven, the cataracts all
	That are open full even, both great and small
	And the planets seven, left have their stall,
	The thunder downdriven, and lightnings now fall
	Full stout,
	On halls and bowers,
	Castles and towers;
	Full sharp are these showers,
	That deluge about.

	Therefore, wife have done, come in the ship fast.
WIFE	Patch your shoes and run, the better they will last.
1ST WIFE	Come, good mother, come, for all is overcast,
	Both the moon and the sun.
2ND WIFE	And many winds blast
	Full sharp;
	These floods may drown our kin,
	Therefore, mother, come in.
WIFE	In faith, still will I spin;
	All in vain ye carp.

3RD WIFE   If ye like, ye may spin, Mother, in the ship.
NOAH   Ye be twice bidden in, dame, in all friendship
WIFE   Whether I lose or I win, in faith, thy fellowship,
           Set I not at a pin, this spindle will I slip
               Upon this hill.
           Ere one foot I stir.
NOAH   By Peter, but ye err;
           Without further spur
               Come in if ye will.

WIFE   Yea, the water nighs so near that I sit not dry,
           Into the ship for fear quickly will I hie
           For dread that I drown here. . . .

NOAH   . . . . Now God help us, we plead!
           As thou art helmsman good, and best may succeed
               Of all;
           Rule us in this race,
           Thy word we embrace.
WIFE   This is a parlous case:
               Help God, when we call.

NOAH   To the tiller, wife, see, and I shall assay
           The deepness of the sea where we sail, if I may.
WIFE   That shall I do full wisely, now go thy way,
           For upon this flood have we fared many a day,
               In pain.
NOAH *lowers a plummet*
NOAH   Now the water will I sound:
           Ah! It is far to the ground;
           This labour I have found
               Brings little gain.
           Above the hills is seen the water risen of late
           Of cubits full fifteen, but in no higher state
           These waves of water green will spill with former
               spate,
           Rain forty days has been, it will therefore abate
               Its zeal.
NOAH *again lowers the plummet*
               Again it is best,

138

The water to test;
Now I am impressed,
    It has waned a great deal.
Now have the storms ceased and cataracts quit,
Both the most and the least.

WIFE   Methinks, by my wit,
The sun shines in the east, lo, is not yond it?
We should have a good feast when these floods flit
    So stormy.

NOAH   We have been here, all we,
Three hundred days and fifty.

WIFE   Yea, look, now wanes the sea;
    Lord, well are we.

NOAH   The third time will I try in what depth we steer.
WIFE   Too long will you ply, lay in thy line there.
NOAH   With my hand touch I the ground even here.
WIFE   Therefore be we spry and have merry cheer;
    But husband,
What hills may there be?

NOAH   Of Armenia's country.
WIFE   Now blessed be he
    That brings us to land!

NOAH   The tops of the hills I see, many at a sight,
Nothing prevents me the sky is so bright.

WIFE   Tokens of mercy these are full right.
NOAH   Dame, now counsel me what bird best might
    Go forth,
With flight of wing
And bring without tarrying
Of mercy some tokening
    Either by south or north?

For this is the first day of the tenth moon.
WIFE   The raven durst I lay will come again soon;
As fast as thou may, cast him forth, have done,
He may come back today and dispel before noon
    Our dismay.

NOAH   I will loose to the blue

Sky, doves one or two:
Go your way, do,
   God send you some prey.

Now have these fowl flown to separate countries;
Let our prayers be known, kneeling on our knees,
To him that is alone worthiest of dignities,
That he may not postpone their coming back to
    please
   Us with a sign.

WIFE   Land they should be gaining,
            The water so is waning.

NOAH   Thank we that God reigning,
            That made both me and mine.

It is a wondrous thing most certainly,
They are so long tarrying, the fowls that we
Cast out in the morning.

WIFE   Sir, it may be
       They bide something to bring.

NOAH   The raven is hungry
         Alway;
       He is without any reason,
       If he find any carrion,
       No matter the season,
          He will not away.

The dove is more gentle, to her trust is due,
Like to the turtle to death she is true.

WIFE   Hence but a little she comes now, look you!
       She brings in her bill some tidings new.
          Behold!
       It is of an olive tree
       A branch, it seems to me.

NOAH   Yea sooth, verily,
            Right so is it called.

Dove, bird full blest, fair might thee befall,
Thou art true to thy quest, as stone in the wall;
Thou wert trusted as best to return to thy hall.

WIFE	A true token to attest we shall be saved all:
	For why?
	The depth, since she has come,
	Of the water by that plumb,
	Hast fallen a fathom
	And more, say I.

1ST SON	These floods are gone, father, behold.
2ND SON	There is left right none, and that be ye bold.
3RD SON	As still as a stone, our ship has firm hold,

NOAH	On land here has run; God's grace is untold;
	My children dear,
	Shem, Japhet, and Ham,
	With glee and with game,
	No longer abide here.

from the Wakefield Mystery Plays

Now read the following:

The Quellers of the Flood

Like the lands of the Bible in the time of Noah, China in ancient times knew the wrath of Heaven in the form of a terrible, all-consuming flood. For long the Yellow Emperor, Ruler of Heaven, had been caused sorrow and anger by the wicked ways of men on earth. At last he came to feel that only the severest punishment would succeed in bringing the mortal world back to its senses, and as the instrument of his punishment he chose to send down torrential, endless flood rains. The cruel and vindictive Spirit of Water, Kung-kung, was placed in charge. Kung-kung carried out his duties without mercy.

First the rain pinned the people in their houses, making it impossible to go out into the fields. Paths turned into quagmires, pools formed in every hollow. Soon, whatever was not under shelter was soaked through and rotted: stacks of grain, piles of fodder, all were useless after a few days of the rain. Holes appeared in the flimsy thatches of huts, and the people shivered and moaned with cold and hunger.

Then, one after another, the rivers broke their banks. The dwellers in the plains and valleys, and all who lived by lake or sea-shore, saw the waters surge towards them or slowly rise at their feet. Many went no farther than the roof of their hut before the waters overtook them. The rest made for the hills, there to seek shelter in caves dug out of the wind-blown soil. Some even copied the birds and made rough nests for themselves in the top-most branches of trees—anything, anywhere to reach a height, to be out of reach of the swirling, menacing waters. Carts and chariots no longer had any value. Everyone wanted a boat, and the boat-builders worked day and night. Every man became a fisherman, for meat was no longer to be had. Every woman searched all day for a tree with leaves or bark on it that her family could eat. And all there was to drink, now that the wells and streams had disappeared, was the brackish, muddy water of the flood itself.

Terrible indeed was the wrath of the Yellow Emperor. But there was one spirit who looked down on the world of men and was moved to pity by their plight. This was Kun, the grandson of the Yellow Emperor, a spirit known to men in the form of a white horse. Kun could not bear to stand idly by and watch such suffering. But when he pleaded with the Ruler of Heaven, his grandfather, to withdraw the flood of his anger, his plea was refused: the measure was not yet full. Kun left the imperial presence and stood wrapped in distress and perplexity.

As he stood there, at a loss, he saw two curious creatures making their way slowly towards him. One was a horned owl, the other was a black tortoise, and they were helping one another along.

'What problem is causing you such distress, great spirit?' asked the owl as the two approached.

'I am filled with pity for the suffering humans,' replied Kun, 'and yet I do not know how their world is to be freed from the great flood.'

'Easy,' grunted the black tortoise. 'All you need is the Magic Mould.'

'The Magic Mould!' exclaimed Kun, astonished. 'What sort of thing is that?'

'It's what I said, it's Magic Mould,' answered the tortoise.

'That's right,' added the owl, helpfully. 'It's what he said. It's mould, you see—earth, soil, you know; and it's magic. That means it can grow, by itself, to any size you want. You only need a little bit. Just get hold of a piece and see for yourself.'

'But where do you get it from?'

'Your grandfather,' said the owl. 'He keeps it.'

Kun's hopes, which had been raised so high, were dashed immediately. 'He would never let me have it,' he sighed.

'Easy,' grunted the black tortoise again. 'Steal it.'

Kun started in alarm, but the owl motioned to him to say nothing, then began to whisper in his ear. The tortoise, too, added a word now and again, and Kun began to nod in agreement with what they were saying. Soon, between the three of them, they had worked out a plan for stealing the Magic Mould from the Yellow Emperor.

Now unfortunately none of the old books tells us just what the plan was; they only tell us that the plan succeeded, so that Kun did in fact lay his hands on a good supply of the precious earth. Although we can't be sure exactly how he did it, it is

clear that a spirit has many advantages when it comes to breaking and entering. However deep in the palace the Magic Mould was hidden, however strong the lock and thick the wall and fierce the guards protecting it, we must remember that Kun had only to change himself into a puff of smoke to get past the guards. Having got past the guards he had only to change himself into a badger to tunnel through the wall; and having tunnelled through the wall he had only to change himself into a tongue of fire to melt the lock on the box which contained the treasure he sought.

As soon as the Magic Mould was in his possession, Kun descended to earth and began his fight against the flood. From a mountain peak he looked down on a broad sheet of water which concealed what had once been a broad and fertile valley. Kun broke off a tiny lump, not much bigger than a pea, from the precious soil he carried, and threw it into the water, ordering it to grow until he told it to stop. The little crumb disappeared beneath the surface. Kun watched. Soon a shadow formed beneath the water; in a little while, it became apparent that the lake bottom was rising. What had been a fathomless lake was now merely a shallow sheet of water. At point after point, soil broke through to the surface—the lake was a marsh, Kun was looking down on a valley floor that was no more than water-logged. Still the Magic Mould grew and grew until all the water was absorbed; and when at last the valley was filled with brown, rich, dry soil, Kun ordered it to stop. Delighted he surveyed his handiwork. Then, from caves on the mountain-sides, poor wretches of human beings came out. Dazed, unbelieving, they looked down on the valley. They had scarcely the strength to cheer, but one after another they stumbled down the hill to touch the good brown earth so magically granted them. And some turned back to their caves to bring out bags of precious seeds which they had guarded through all their vicissitudes, and which now at last they could sow.

Cyril Birch

(The story does not end here. Kun travels throughout the length and breadth of the land, filling the valleys so that 'wherever he cast his Magic Mould the flood waters were soaked up as though by some giant sponge', but he is punished by the Yellow Emperor for his disobedience—he is killed by the cruel Spirit of Fire. But while his body is dead, Kun's spirit lives on in the Chinese Dragon that eventually wins freedom for the people. The full version of this story can be found in *Chinese Myths and Fantasies*, published by the Oxford University Press.)

Discussion

Compare the three versions of this event you have read, discussing how they differ and what they have in common. Why, do you think, have different civilizations had this story in their heritage?

Action

Create a drama from this extract.

1 In the same groups as in the Noah play, improvise scenes that will dramatize the effects of each stage of the story on a Chinese family. First of all imagine their life before the flood, and then, using the details that emerge here, give as realistic a picture as you can of the suffering at the hands of Kung-kung, and their 'dazed, unbelieving' return to life and hope as a result of the mercy of Kun.

2 Further groups can improvise
   a the scene in which the Yellow Emperor comes to his decision to punish 'the wicked ways of men on earth' and his instructions to Kung-kung;
   b the scene between Kun and his grandfather the Yellow Emperor, when Kun's plea for mercy is refused;
   c Kun's meeting with the Owl and the Tortoise;
   d Kun's seizure of the Magic Mould. For this scene you will probably need a narrator, as well as the guards.

e The Yellow Emperor, Kung-kung and Kun should make masks for themselves or wear stylized make-up to differentiate themselves from the mortals. How are you going to suggest the Owl and the Tortoise?

3 Work out movement to enact the effects of Kung-kung's action, and those of Kun's distribution of the Magic Mould. (You will be able to adapt ideas you used in the Greek version of this story earlier in this Chapter.)

4 Use a group of readers for the narrators and another group of musicians—playing, for instance, cymbals and drums—to provide a background for the action you worked out in **3**.

5 Fit together the best improvisations in **1** with the other elements in **2** and **3** for a performance of this story.

5 Creation

I stretch beyond the bounds of the world,
I'm smaller than a worm, outstrip the sun,
I shine more brightly than the moon. The swelling seas,
the fair face of the earth and all the green fields,
are within my clasp. I cover the depths,
and plunge beneath hell; I ascend above heaven,
highland of renown; I reach beyond
the boundaries of the land of blessed angels.
I fill far and wide
all the corners of the earth and the ocean streams.
How can you tell me what my name is?
    Anglo-Saxon Riddle, translated by Kevin Crossley-Holland

A Spring

Composition and Discussion

The following poem vividly describes a walk in snow made by
the poet when he was a very small child:

After Christmas

It was later than Christmas
    a January snow as round as
        sparrows eggs
    fell like feathers, and I was knee-high
        glad that it was so

It was later than Christmas
    and no-one in the half-dark world
        as long as
    a year and a year to go was there
        to share a thing

It was only my mother
    my father and myself stepped high
        and slowly where
    the winter year began to flow
        in feathered January

It was only my first
    and now my only memory; the year
        began and ended then
    in January, in darkness, and
        in snow

It was later than Christmas
    and when Christmas had come round again
        the snow had gone
    and there were merely years repeating
        what was known.

Edwin Brock

1 Discuss the effects of the rhythm of the poem and the way the poet repeats phrases. The poem seems to move in slow motion as if the memory haunts him. Perhaps you have a similar experience that you would like to capture in words as Edwin Brock has done here.

2 Alternatively, write about the deadness of winter: perhaps with everything under snow, perhaps not—but try to convey the sense of life coiled in roots and fur, waiting for the sun to draw it out again.

In early spring notice carefully how everything comes to life almost imperceptibly: make accurate notes on the way buds form, their texture and the way they burst into flower; the sharp greenness of the new leaves, the way they uncurl. Really watch the way hedgerows and gardens change colour—watch as you have never done before, as if seeing the glory of spring for the first time. Build your notes into a careful, detailed description of the changing scene.

3 Compare what the poets in the following two poems have to say about spring. Don't confine yourself to studying the words you can see printed on the page before you, but read them aloud to add the greater dimension of sound and rhythm. Use your ears as well as your eyes to understand them, and notice carefully the different ways in which the poets have arranged their words and the effect of these arrangements.

Spring

Nothing is so beautiful as spring—
    When weeds, in wheels, shoot long and lovely and lush;
    Thrush's eggs look little low heavens, and thrush
Through the echoing timber does so rinse and wring
The ear, it strikes like lightnings to hear him sing;
    The glassy peartree leaves and blooms, they brush
    The descending blue; that blue is all in a rush
With richness; the racing lambs too have fair their fling.

Gerard Manley Hopkins

April Rise

If ever I saw blessing in the air
    I see it now in this still early day
Where lemon-green the vaporous morning drips
    Wet sunlight on the powder of my eye.

Blown bubble-film of blue, the sky wraps round
    Weeds of warm light whose every root and rod
Splutters with soapy green, and all the world
    Sweats with the bead of summer in its bud.

If ever I heard blessing it is there
    Where birds in trees that shoals and shadows are
Splash with their hidden wings and drops of sound
    Break on my ears their crests of throbbing air.

Pure in the haze the emerald sun dilates,
    The lips of sparrows milk the mossy stones,
While white as water by the lake a girl
    Swims her green hand among the gathered swans.

Now, as the almond burns its smoking wick,
  Dropping small flames to light the candled grass;
Now, as my low blood scales its second chance,
  If ever world were blessed, now it is.

Laurie Lee

4 Get to know these poems well: read them many times on
days in spring when it feels good to be alive, when the blood
tingles through your veins and the weather makes you feel
that you can achieve anything, when everything around you
is so clear it seems almost strange and new. Enjoy the
sounds these poems make: read them aloud often.

5 Write your own poem about this kind of day and the powerful feelings it rouses in you, making clear what exactly it is
in the spring day that excites you, so that in his imagination
the reader can see, hear and smell this special day.

B A windy day

This wind brings all dead things to life,
Branches that lash the air like whips
And dead leaves rolling in a hurry
Or peering in a rabbit's bury
Or trying to push down a tree;
Gates that fly open to the wind
And close again behind,
And fields that are a flowing sea
And make the cattle look like ships;
Straws glistening and stiff
Lying on air as on a shelf,
And pond that leaps to leave itself;
And feathers too that rise and float
Each feather changed into a bird,

And line-hung sheets that crack and strain;
Even the sun-greened coat,
That through so many winds has served,
The scarecrow struggles to put on again.

Andrew Young

Action

In groups rehearse the above poem for performance to the rest of the class, having discussed how you are going to divide the lines between you.

Composition

1 On a windy day go outside and notice carefully the wind's effects on you. Notice the way it pulls at you, your skin, eyes, clothes; raise your arms and feel its power lifting you; run against it, and then turn with your back to it.

2 Now watch the way it tosses trees, telephone lines, litter. Watch how birds use the wind, and its effects on their wings and feathers. Observe its effects on other people as well. Watch the racing clouds. Notice every detail of the scene, as Glyn Hughes has here:

Along its nervous shore
curlews crouch, farmers shudder to a fire

each ear pressed to a shell
listening to the crash of clouds'

tall cleft chimneys. No sheep can hide,
no field can tilt away,

yet it has torn all day
reaching like a mind

tugged by vision into clothes and quarries
with volleys of rain that cannot rest

till they reach the unyielding walls
of farms and barns,

mills a million little-eyed
and knuckles of rock in the peat

cut by the keening wind
like bollards around which ropes have strained.

It rakes the thistles together, bangs
a tin in a gap. Although sometimes

sunlight cuts out squares
and butchers the land,

it has blown blue shifting glooms
to almost every place.

3 Listen to the wind at night, echoing through chimneys and
rafters, scattering dustbin lids, whining among trees . . .
really *listen* to all the sounds it makes.

4 Make accurate descriptions of all you experience, then
select material from your descriptions for a poem about a
Windy Day or Night. Make the rhythm of your poem and
the force of your words help express the wind's violence.

5 The following poems were written by people of your age.
Compare their images with yours.

a It came upon me. I could not stop it
Clutching me in its icy grip.
Little tingles like money spiders
Ran up and down my spine.

My hair waved in a wild confusion,
My clothes seemed to tear away.
It clamped upon my eyes like vices,
And whistled in my ears and said,

'Sleep on, and on, sleep in silent slumber.'
It held me up as if on a bed.
Everything was of no importance,
And my mind began to reel.

I had broken the laws of aviation.
I was floating, floating, floating.
I could have slept, and gone on sleeping
Until the warmth of the classroom.

William

b The rose bush shudders
The wind is coming
Leaves winding and whirling
Twirling and swirling

It buffets me along
My hair covers my face
The twigs dancing in glee
And gloating at the wind

The puffy clouds sail along
And then suddenly charge across the sky
My clothes press against my back
And then they are released

Bridget

c So strong that it sends you flying forward.
Then, suddenly, it is back, stronger than before,
The trees bending and swaying
Like grass being trampled on.

Rushing over the buildings
Like an express down the track,
The telephone wires twanging
As the wind strikes them.

John

d Light filters through the slowly sifting clouds.
Trees, knobbly-kneed, strain against the wicked wind.
Muscles tighten against its shifts, and dead leaves
Jump, scarves buckle and fold, hair flows,
Clothes struggle. And the menace still comes on.

Graham

e The howling hiss of the crawling wind
Scatters my dry hair into my face
And over my blood-red ears.
This mighty torrent has the trees at its
Menacing mutinous mercy,
Clasping with its outstretched claws.
I clench my knuckled fists, run to
Escape. Suddenly a weakness seems to
Echo through the Wind's jostling mind.
Silently I sigh as it soars away skybound.

David

C Heaven and earth and man

Here is another Chinese myth that, again, makes fascinating comparison with the Bible:

Earth with its mountains, rivers and seas, Sky with its sun, moon and stars: in the beginning all these were one, and the one was Chaos. Nothing had taken shape, all was a dark swirling confusion, over and under, round and round. For countless ages this was the way of the universe, unformed and unillumined, until from the midst of Chaos came P'an Ku. Slowly, slowly, he grew into being, feeding on the elements, eyes closed, sleeping a sleep of eighteen thousand years. At last the moment came when he woke from his sleeping. He opened his eyes: nothing could he see, nothing but darkness, nothing but confusion. In his anger he raised his great arm and struck out blindly in the face of the murk, and with one great crashing blow he scattered the elements of Chaos.

The swirling ceased, and in its place came a new kind of movement. No longer confined, all those things which were light in weight and pure in nature rose upwards; all those things which were heavy and gross sank down. With his one mighty blow P'an Ku had freed sky from earth.

Now P'an Ku stood with his feet on earth, and the sky rested on his head. So long as he stood between the two they could not come together again. And as he stood, the rising and the sinking went on. With each day that passed the earth grew thicker by ten feet and the sky rose higher by ten feet, thrust even farther from the earth by P'an Ku's body which daily grew in height by ten feet also. For eighteen thousand years more P'an Ku continued to grow until his own body was gigantic, and until earth was formed of massive thickness and the sky had risen far above. Thousands of miles tall he stood, a great pillar separating earth from sky so that the two might never again come together to dissolve once more into a single Chaos. Throughout long ages he stood, until the time when he could be sure that earth and sky were fixed and firm in their places.

When this time came, P'an Ku, his task achieved, lay down on earth to rest, and resting died. And now he, who in his life had brought shape to the universe, by his death gave his body to make it rich and beautiful. He gave the breath from his body to form the winds and clouds, his voice to be the rolling thunder, his two eyes to be the sun and moon, the hairs of his head and beard to be the stars, the sweat of his brow to be the rain and dew. To the earth he gave his body for the mountains and his hands and feet for the two poles and the extremes of east and west. His blood flowed as the rivers of earth and his veins ran as the roads which cover the land. His flesh became the soil of the fields and the hairs of his body grew on as the flowers and trees. As for his bones and teeth, these sank deep below the surface of earth to enrich it as precious metals.

And so P'an Ku brought out of Chaos the heavens in all their glory and the earth with all its splendours.

But although the earth could now present its lovely landscapes, although beasts ran in its forests and fish swam in its

158

rivers, still it seemed to lack something, something which would make it less empty and dull for the gods who came down from Heaven to roam over its surface. One day the goddess Nü-kua, whose body was that of a dragon but whose head was of human form, grew weary of the loneliness of earth. After long thought she stooped and took from the ground a lump of clay. From this she fashioned with her dragon claws a tiny creature. The head she shaped after the pattern of her own, but to the body she gave two arms and two legs. She set the little thing back on the ground: and the first human being came to life and danced and made sounds of joy to delight the eyes and ears of the goddess. Quickly she made many more of these charming humans, and felt lonely no longer as they danced together all about her.

Then, as she rested a while from her task and watched the sons and daughters of her own creation go off together across the earth, a new thought came to her. What would become of the world when all these humans she had made grew old and died? They were fine beings, well fitted to rule over the beasts of the earth; but they would not live for ever. To fill the earth with humans, then when these had gone to make more to take their place, this would mean an endless task for the goddess. And so to solve this problem Nü-kua brought together man and woman and taught them the ways of marriage. Now they could create for themselves their own sons and daughters, and these in turn could continue to people the earth throughout time.

After this gift of marriage from Nü-kua, further blessings came to man from her husband, the great god Fu-hsi. He again had a human head but the body of a dragon. He taught men how to weave ropes to make nets for fishing, and he made the lute from which men first drew music. His also was the priceless gift of fire. Men had seen and feared the fire which was struck from the forest trees by the passing of the Lord of the Thunderstorm. But Fu-hsi, who was the son of this same lord, taught men to drill wood against wood and make fire for their own use, for warmth and for cooking.

Already the creatures of Nü-kua's making could speak their thoughts to one another, but Fu-hsi now drew for them the eight precious symbols with which they could begin to make records for those who were to come after. He drew three strokes

≡ to represent Heaven; the three strokes broken ☷ represented earth. That symbol whose middle stroke was solid ☵ represented water, that whose middle stroke was broken ☲ represented fire. A solid stroke above ☶ gave the sign for mountains, a solid stroke beneath ☳ the sign for storms; a broken line below ☴ showed wind, a broken line on top ☱ showed marshland. With these eight powerful symbols man could begin to record all he observed of the world about him.

For long years men lived their lives in a world at peace. Then, suddenly, there spread from Heaven to earth a conflict which threatened to put an end to all creation. This was the battle between the Spirit of Water, Kung-kung, and the Spirit of Fire, Chu-jung. Down to earth came the turbulent, wilful Kung-kung to whip up huge waves on river and lake and lead his scaly hordes against his arch-enemy, Fire. Chu-jung fought back with tongues of flame and scorching breath and halted the rebel Water in his path. Kung-kung's armies dispersed and he, their leader, turned and fled. But his flight brought with it a peril greater yet. For, dashing blindly off to the west, Kung-kung struck his head against the mountain Pu-chou-shan, which was none other than the pillar that in the western corner held up the sky.

Kung-kung made good his escape, but he left the world in a disastrous state. Great holes appeared in the sky, whilst the earth tilted up in the west. In that region deep cracks and fissures appeared, which are still to be seen to this day. All the rivers and lakes spilled out their waters, which ran off and still run eastwards: off to the south-east, where the earth had slipped down low, ran the waters together to form a vast ocean there. Meanwhile, out of the shaken mountain forests, fire still raged forth, and wild beasts of every kind left their lairs to maraud through the world of helpless, terrified men.

It was left to the goddess Nü-kua to bring back order to the world, to quell the fire and flood and tame the wandering beasts. She it was also who selected from the beds of rivers stones of the most perfect colouring. These she heated until they could be moulded, then with these stones, block by block, she patched the holes in the sky. Lastly, she killed a giant turtle, and cut off its powerful legs to make pillars between which the sky is firmly held over the earth, never again to fall.

So the peace of the world was restored. But the mountains still rise in the west, and it is to there that the sun, moon and stars still run down the tilted sky; whilst to the east, the waters of the earth still gather into the restless ocean.

Cyril Birch

Action

1 Work out a dance drama to convey the movement of this story:
   a the 'swirling confusion' of Chaos
   b the effects on nature of P'an Ku's growth and death
   c Nü-kua's creation
   d the war between fire and water
   e the restoration of peace.
2 Use narrated extracts from this account and percussion or music like Stravinsky's *Rite of Spring* as a background to your drama.
3 Think of how you can make a visual impact from the use of symbols painted on shields or banners—the symbols for fire, water, wind mentioned in the story, for instance.
4 Earth, Fire, Water, Wind: you have written about all of these elements. Weave extracts from them into a programme called *Heaven and Earth and Man*.

Suggestions for further reading

Joan Aiken: Black Hearts in Battersea; Nightbirds on Nantucket; The Whispering Mountain; The Wolves of Willoughby Chase.

William Armstrong: Sounder.

John Christopher: The White Mountains; The City of Gold and Lead; The Pool of Fire; Prince in Waiting; Beyond the Burning Lands.

Catherine Cookson: Joe and the Gladiator.

Peter Dickinson: The Weathermonger; Heartsease; The Devil's Children.

Gerald Durrell: The New Noah (and other books about animals).

J. Meade Falkner: Moonfleet.

Leon Garfield: Mr. Corbett's Ghost; Devil-in-the-Fog; Jack Holborn; Smith; The Drummer-Boy.

Alan Garner: Elidor; The Moon of Gomrath; The Weirdstone of Brisingham.

John Gordon: The Giant under Snow.

Roger Lancelyn Green: King Arthur and His Knights of the Round Table; Myths of the Norsemen.

Frederick Grice: The Bonny Pit Laddie.

Meindert de Jong: Shadrach; The Tower by the Sea.

Ursula Leguin: The Wizard of Earthsea; The Tombs of Atuan.

C. S. Lewis: Narnia Chronicle.

Reginald Maddock: The Big Ditch; Northmen's Fury.

James Vance Marshall: Walkabout.

William Mayne: Earthfasts.

Bill Naughton: The Goalkeeper's Revenge and other Stories.

Andre Norton: The Beast Master and other S.F. Stories, especially the trilogy Sargasso of Space; Plague Ship; Postmarked the Stars.

Mary Patchett: The Brumby.

Philippa Pearce: A Dog so Small.

James Reeves: The Cold Flame.

Andrew Salkey: Earthquake; Hurricane.

Jack Schaefer: Shane.

Ian Seraillier: Beowulf the Warrior; The Silver Sword; The Way of Danger.

David Severn: The Future Took Us.

Neville Shute: Pied Piper.

Ivan Southall: Ash Road; Hills End.

John Steinbeck: The Red Pony.

Rosemary Sutcliff: Dragon-Slayer; The Story of Beowulf; Dawn Wind; The Lantern Bearers; Tristram and Iseult.

J. Tolkien: The Hobbit; The Lord of the Rings.

Mart Treadgold: We Couldn't Leave Dinah.

Henry Treese: Vikings Dawn; Vikings Sunset; Horned Helmet; The Road to Miklagaard; Vinland the Good.

Mark Twain: Tom Sawyer; Huckleberry Finn.

Jill Paton Walsh: Fireweed.

Rex Warner: Men and Gods.

Barbara Willard: The Sprig of Broom.

Kenneth Ulyatt: North against the Sioux.

Acknowledgments

The drawings in *The Quest* are by Paul Newland.

The Publishers' thanks are due to the following for permission to reproduce copyright material:
Mrs. G. Redwood-Anderson for John Redwood-Anderson's poem 'Spurn Light'; Oxford University Press for extracts from Cyril Birch's *Chinese Myths and Fantasies* and Rosemary Sutcliff's *The Lantern Bearers*; Scorpion press for 'After Christmas' from Edwin Brock's *An Attempt at Exorcism*; David Higham Associates Ltd for Charles Causley's 'Nelson Gardens'; Macmillan & Co. Ltd for Kevin Crossley-Holland's poem 'Creation' from *Storm*, Wilfred Gibson's poem 'Flannan Isle' from *Collected Poems* by permission of Mr. M. Gibson and Glyn Hughes' poem 'Wind' from *Neighbours*; David

Higham Associates Ltd for Ronald Duncan's 'September and October'; J. M. Dent & Sons Ltd for Clifford Dyment's poem 'The Singing Sailor' from *Straight or Curley*; Longman Young Books Ltd for an extract from *Jack Holborn* by Leon Garfield; Wm Collins Sons & Co. Ltd for two extracts from Alan Garner's *The Moon of Gomrath*; Faber & Faber Ltd for an extract from William Golding's *Lord of the Flies* and Theodore Roethke's poem 'The Storm' from *The Collected Poems of Theodore Roethke*; Michael Joseph Ltd for an extract from *A Kestrel for a Knave* by Barry Hines; Mr. Laurie Lee for his two poems 'Field of Autumn' and 'April Rise'; The Hogarth Press for an extract from Laurie Lee's *Cider with Rosie* and Norman MacCaig's poem 'Summer Farm' from *Riding Lights*; the Viking Press for Sean O'Faolain's story 'The Trout'; Faber & Faber Ltd for 'The First Day at School' from William Saroyan's *Little Children*; Mr. Vernon Scannell for his poem 'Hide and Seek'; Angus & Robertson (U.K.) Ltd for an extract from Ivan Southall's *Ash Road*; Mrs. Myfanwy Thomas for Edward Thomas's poems 'Cock-Crow' and 'After Rain'; Mac-Gibbon and Kee Ltd for 'The Great Flood' from Rex Warner's *Men and Gods* and Rupert Hart-Davis for Andrew Young's poems 'The Sheaf' and 'A Windy Day' from *Collected Poems*.

We would also like to thank the following for permission to reprint copyright photographs and other material (page numbers in brackets):
J. Allan Cash (opposite 1, 22, 24, 30, 32, 34, 38, 60, 64, 65 bottom, 66, 111, 115, 125); Australian News & Information Bureau (71); Peter Baker (35); Barnaby's Picture Library (18, 41, 58, 75, 116, 150); Bob Collins (9, 23, 49, 57); Richard Gee (11, 51); Greater London Council (65 top); Sarah Hobson (13, 148); The Hogarth Press (44); Raymond Irons (frontispiece, 33, 90, 97, 121, 123); Noeline Kelly (12); Keystone Press Agency (23, 95, 113, 118, 127); National Film Archive (21); Tom Parker (114); Radio Times Hulton Picture Library (103, 104, 105, 107); Spectrum (7, 31, 36, 39, 53, 109, 152); Malcolm Roberton (28).